the depleted self

the depleted self

sin in a narcissistic age

DONALD CAPPS

FORTRESS PRESS + MINNEAPOLIS

THE DEPLETED SELF
Sin in a Narcissistic Age

Scripture quotations unless otherwise noted are from the New Revised Standard Version of the Bible, copyright © 1989 by the Division of Christian Education of the National Council of the Churches of Christ in the United States.

Excerpts from *Diagnostic and Statistical Manual of Mental Disorders, Third Edition, Revised,* copyright © 1987 American Psychiatric Association, are reprinted by permission.

Excerpts from *Borderline Conditions and Pathological Narcissism* by Otto Kernberg, copyright © 1975 Jason Aronson, Inc., are reprinted by permission of the publisher.

Excerpts from *Authority* by Richard Sennett, copyright © 1980 by Richard Sennett, are reprinted by permission of Alfred A. Knopf, Inc., and International Creative Management, Inc.

Excerpts from *The Culture of Narcissism: American Life in an Age of Diminishing Expectations* by Christopher Lasch (New York: W. W. Norton & Co., 1978) are reprinted by permission of the publisher.

Interior design: James F. Brisson
Cover design: James F. Brisson

Library of Congress Cataloging-in-Publication Data

Capps, Donald.
    The depleted self : sin in a narcissistic age / Donald Capps.
        p.   cm.
    Includes bibliographical references and index.
    ISBN 0-8006-2587-0 (alk. paper)
    1. Sin.   2. Narcissism.   3. Guilt.   4. Shame.   I. Title.
BT715.C27   1993
241'.3—dc20   92-7931
                                                                    CIP

The paper used in this publication meets the minimum requirements of American National Standard for Information Sciences—Permanence of Paper for Printed Library Materials, ANSI Z329.48-1984.   ∞ ™

Manufactured in the U.S.A.   AF 1-2587

97   2   3   4   5   6   7   8   9   10

Contents

Acknowledgments

In 1990 I delivered the Schaff Lectures at Pittsburgh Theological Seminary. An expectation of Schaff lecturers is that they will publish their lectures; this book is my effort to fulfill that expectation. I deeply appreciate the stimulus that the lectureship afforded me to address the issues discussed in this book, and the warm and spirited reception that I received from faculty, students, pastors, and laity who attended the lectures. My special thanks to President Samuel Calian for his gracious hospitality, and to Andrew Purves and Martha Robbins, Pittsburgh Theological Seminary's professors in the pastoral theology field, both of whom welcomed me with open arms, and, through their supportive comments and questions, caused me to feel that these lectures were worth the wider dissemination that the publication of this book will now make possible.

I also want to thank my colleague and friend, Richard K. Fenn, Professor of Christianity and Society at Princeton Theological Seminary, who has helped me formulate and refine my thinking about the issues discussed in this book, and, in the process, has shared his own ideas and insights, knowing that many of them would find their way into print here.

My friend, Owe Wikstrom, Professor of the Psychology of Religion at Uppsala University in Sweden, provided the initial impetus for this book by arranging for me to receive an honorary doctorate in theology from Uppsala University in 1989. My lecture on this occasion was on the subject of narcissism and sin. One of the auditors of this lecture was Agne Nordlander, Principal of Johannelunds Theological Institute in Uppsala, who, on hearing of my desire to return to Sweden for a more leisurely visit, provided my wife and me a guest room at the Institute and invited me to lecture on the same theme at a three-day conference for theological students and pastors on the Christian response to the contemporary world, held at the Institute in October 1990. To Professor Wikstrom and Principal Nordlander my heartfelt thanks for their interest in my work and their assurances that what I had to say about narcissism and sin related as much to their society as to my own.

I also want to note my special indebtedness to Richard Hutch. When I was a very new professor at the University of Chicago in the early 70s, Dick took a chance on me, and wrote his doctoral dissertation on Ralph Waldo Emerson under my direction. In returning to Emerson's work in the writing of this book, I had fond recollections of Dick's and my conversations about Emerson. As I came to Emerson through his eyes, his influence on this book is incalculable.

In a similar way, my conversations with Brad A. Binau, who wrote his doctoral dissertation at Princeton Theological Seminary under my direction on shame and the sacrament of baptism, have provided considerable insight for me on the issues discussed in chapter 4. Also, his article on shame and the human predicament has been of particular value to me in my own efforts to think about shame within a theological frame of reference.[1] I have also had fruitful discussions on shame with Nelson Ould, a doctoral student at the University of Edinburgh who spent the 1991–92 academic year at Princeton Theological Seminary, and Susan L. Nelson, a professor of theology at Pittsburgh Theological Seminary, who has shared with me her own unpublished work on a theology of shame. I am deeply indebted to these three conversation partners who have shared freely of their ideas with me

---

1. Brad A. Binau, "Shame and the Human Predicament," in *Counseling and the Human Predicament*, ed. LeRoy Aden and David G. Benner (Grand Rapids: Baker Book House, 1989), 127–43.

and have confirmed for me the vital importance of this line of theological inquiry.

My appreciation, also, to Timothy G. Staveteig, of Augsburg Fortress Press, who is responsible for this book finding its way into print, to David Lott, who supervised the production of the book, and to Gary Lee, whose copyediting significantly improved the book in substance as well as form. John Capps prepared the index.

I have dedicated this book to another good friend, Frederick F. Lansill, Vice-President for Financial Affairs at Princeton Theological Seminary. Through his cheerful, slightly off-center perspective on life, and his ability to be of genuine help to individuals, Rick has demonstrated that an institution can be responsive to human needs and aspirations. The dedication of this book to him is a small token of thanks in my own behalf, and in behalf of the many others whom he has befriended through the years.

Abbreviations

AS   Heinz Kohut, *The Analysis of the Self: A Systematic Approach to the Psychoanalytic Treatment of Narcissistic Personality Disorders.* New York: International Universities Press, 1971.

Auth   Richard Sennett, *Authority.* New York: Alfred A. Knopf, 1980.

BCPN   Otto Kernberg, *Borderline Conditions and Pathological Narcissism.* Northvale, N.J.: Jason Aronson, 1975.

CN   Christopher Lasch, *The Culture of Narcissism: American Life in an Age of Diminishing Expectations.* New York: Warner Books, 1979.

CS   Erik H. Erikson, *Childhood and Society.* 2d ed. New York: W. W. Norton, 1963.

DSTT   Heinz Kohut and Ernest S. Wolf, "The Disorders of the Self and Their Treatment: An Outline." In *EPN,* 175–96.

EPN   Andrew P. Morrison, ed. *Essential Papers on Narcissism.* New York: New York Univ. Press, 1986.

ERMT   Paul Tillich, "Estrangement and Reconciliation in Modern Thought." In *MH,* 1–15.

HH Robert N. Bellah, Richard Madsen, William M. Sullivan, Ann Swidler, and Steven M. Tipton, *Habits of the Heart: Individualism and Commitment in American Life*. Berkeley: Univ. of California Press, 1985.

MH Perry Lefevre, ed. *The Meaning of Health: Essays in Existentialism, Psychoanalysis, and Religion*. Chicago: Exploration Press, 1984.

NPT Ben Bursten, "Some Narcissistic Personality Types." In *EPN*, 377–402.

RS Heinz Kohut, *The Restoration of the Self*. New York: International Universities Press, 1977.

SR Ralph Waldo Emerson, "Self-Reliance." In *The Essays of Ralph Waldo Emerson*, 25–51. Cambridge, Mass.: The Belknap Press of Harvard Univ. Press, 1987.

SS Michael P. Nichols, *The Self in the System: Expanding the Limits of Family Therapy*. New York: Brunner/Mazel, 1987.

WBHN Paul Tillich, "What Is Basic in Human Nature?" In *MH*, 184–91.

the depleted self

1

Whatever Became of Sin?

Over the past few years, sin has not been a central topic of interest within the pastoral care and counseling field. A major contribution of the pastoral counseling movement of the 1950s was its challenge of the clergy's tendency to address parishioners' problems in a moralistic fashion instead of exploring these problems in their psychodynamic context. Leaders of the pastoral counseling movement argued that, when ministers give appropriate attention to psychodynamic issues, their attitude toward parishioners is much more likely to be one of understanding and genuine concern, not moralistic and judgmental. Parishioners will be viewed less as sinners rebelling against the laws of God and human nature, and more as victims, caught in a complex set of personal circumstances and psychosocial conditions over which they may exercise only limited influence and control.

Furthermore, the pastoral care field has emphasized that positive change does not normally result from criticizing or condemning individuals for their behavior, however inappropriate or misguided such behavior may seem to an outside observer, but by accepting these individuals, and communicating through attitude and words that they are unconditionally prized and valued. Thus, even though the pastoral care and counseling movement has recognized the sinfulness of humankind, it has shown great reluctance to charge individuals with sin, or to assert their sin-fulness, as this is considered counterproductive.

Risking the Red Flag of Sin

Given the recent history of the pastoral care and counseling movement, and its impressive contributions toward the realization of a more enlightened, psychologically aware, and considerably less moralistic clergy, the very idea of a book on sin written by someone in this field is likely to raise many red flags, especially the fear that even broaching the subject may be a small but fatal step backward into the dark ages from which our predecessors worked so hard and tirelessly to free us. To say that sin is not a popular topic among my colleagues is an understatement. If some of the pioneers of the movement talked about sin, usually in discussions about guilt and guilt feelings, and explored the anxiety produced by feelings of guilt, their successors have had virtually nothing to say about sin.

Also, even though we are witnessing new interest in pastoral care and counseling among conservatives and evangelicals, the vast majority have been attracted to this field because they share the view of their more liberal counterparts that pastors' tendency to moralize within the counseling process needs to be replaced by a deeper awareness of psychodynamic processes and greater knowledge of systemic models of human interaction. Jay E. Adams, the one conservative for whom sin is the central theme of his work, is the exception who proves the rule, and most conservatives and evangelicals find his views extreme, even dangerous, when applied.

Even to broach the subject of sin is to risk rejection or dismissal by colleagues in the pastoral care and counseling field. Some would say that this is hardly a realistic fear (for, after all, a number of colleagues have recently made a strong case for the revival of "moral discourse" in pastoral care), but there is a major difference between a call for greater attention to the "moral context" of pastoral care and the call for serious and sustained attention to sin. To argue for the recovery of moral discourse in pastoral care and counseling is certainly to recognize that we need to do more than focus on psychodynamics and psychosocial processes. But to call for increased attention to the "moral context" of pastoral care, as Don S. Browning and other ethicists have done, is not yet to have addressed the matter of sin, which is, after all, a theological matter.

Another problem involved in writing a book on sin today is that one cannot simply draw on the achievements of the pioneers in pastoral theology, for their views on sin are no longer adequate. Our sociocultural situation today is significantly, if not radically, different from that confronted by these pioneers, such as Anton Boisen, Seward Hiltner, Carroll Wise, Wayne Oates, and Howard Clinebell. We cannot simply engage in an exercise of retrieval, by resurrecting, for example, what these pioneers had to say about sin and forgiveness. While I hope to show that sin language is as relevant to the human situation as it ever was, I do not believe that we can ignore the fact that something has changed, perhaps radically, in the way that we today experience a sense of wrongness—wrongness in our inner selves, wrongness in our relations with other persons, and wrongness in our relations with God.

In our times, we are much more likely to experience this "wrongfulness" according to shame, rather than guilt, dynamics. Thus, to speak meaningfully and relevantly about sin, we have to relate sin to the experience of shame—not only, not even primarily, to the experience of guilt. Obviously, this will involve a reformulation of our theology of sin, a reformulation that is so deep and extensive that it calls for a fundamental change in our theological paradigm. Black, feminist, and Third World theologians have laid the foundations for this paradigm shift by emphasizing the need to theologize from the perspective of the victim, but no one has addressed in a systematic way the specific problem of how to reflect on sin within a cultural milieu in which shame, not guilt, is the predominant experience, the more deeply felt emotion.

Noting the Narcissistic Self

The human reality that has been emerging for at least two decades now is a new type of individual—or self—for whom the traditional language of guilt, and traditional distinctions between guilt and guilt feelings, or real and neurotic guilt, no longer has much relevance. To the extent that sin language has depended on individuals' capacity to experience guilt, the fact that guilt is no longer a central human experience poses a very difficult problem for pastoral theologians who believe that it is essential to take sin seriously, and to recover the ability to talk about sin in an intelligent, perceptive, and genuinely helpful manner.

Contemporary theology has, in general, failed to recognize the threat that this new type of individual or self, usually labeled "narcissist," poses for traditional theological language. Or perhaps contemporary theology has understood the threat it poses for traditional theological language all too well; this would account for the fact that theologians of every stripe have denounced this new type of self rather than attempted to understand it. Theologians have not read what psychologists and psychotherapists have written about the narcissistic self, but have, instead, been content to take their cues from moralists like Robert N. Bellah and his coauthors of *Habits of the Heart*, which inveighs against our individualistic age, but lacks an in-depth understanding of the narcissistic self, an understanding that is easily accessible from psychological and psychotherapeutic writings on this phenomenon. Also, such denunciations of narcissism by theologians rarely include any acknowledgment that the narcissism label does not only apply to others, but applies to all of us, regardless of age, gender, or social status. Therefore, one of the goals in this book is to make the writings by the psychological community on narcissism more accessible to the theological community. Otherwise, the theological community will succumb to a moralistic attitude that is as unhelpful as the moralism against which the pastoral counseling movement fought so vigorously in the 1950s.

Many readers will recall Karl Menninger's book, *Whatever Became of Sin,* which was published in 1973.[1] This book struck a responsive chord among many pastors who were concerned about the absence or devaluation of sin language in American society, especially among the mainline Protestant churches. That the question, Whatever became of sin? was posed by a highly esteemed psychiatrist, one known for his tireless efforts to decriminalize mental illness, was an important reason why the question did not fall on unresponsive ears. After all, Menninger was not a fundamentalist preacher, but a member of the psychiatric community, and psychiatry had been one of the pastoral counseling movement's major allies in its efforts to overcome the moralistic framework of much of what had previously passed for pastoral care.

But the enthusiasm that greeted Menninger's book did not last for long; now, ironically, we are forced to ask the same question: Whatever became of sin? One reason that Menninger's appeal for the revival of sin language did not have any lasting effect is that he did not address the deep and pervasive psychocultural reasons why sin seems to have so little meaning for us today. He complains about our reluctance, as a society and as individuals, to accept responsibility for our corporate and personal actions, but he does not have a clearly formulated theory about how or why we got this way. Thus, rather than providing an explanation for this situation, he ends up criticizing and moralizing about it. As a result, his book comes across as the preachings of a frustrated man who observes the present situation, is deeply troubled by it, but can only rail against it. A deep ambivalence also runs through the book; Menninger wants to be sure that his call for greater attention to sin will not play into the hands of those who would turn back the clock and recriminalize mental illness and deviant adolescent behavior. Thus, even as he calls for renewed attention to sin with his right hand, his left hand tends subtly to undermine this call.

1. Karl Menninger, *Whatever Became of Sin?* (New York: Hawthorn Books, 1973).

Menninger needed to situate his call for a recovery of sin language within a careful analysis of the contemporary self, as this self has taken shape in the latter half of the twentieth century. Had he done so, he would have been able to explain why, for example, "the great sin" of his own youth—the sin of masturbation—is no longer considered a great sin today. Instead of merely noting and lamenting that sin language is no longer popular, he would have provided an explanation for this development. It is especially ironic that a psychiatrist did not make use of the evidence that was available to him—evidence being generated by his own psychiatry staff at the Menninger Foundation, among other places—that a new self, with all its possibilities as well as aberrations, had come onto the scene. (One of the major psychoanalytic interpreters of this new self, Otto Kernberg, did his exploratory work at the Menninger Foundation, and his influential book, *Borderline Conditions and Pathological Narcissism*, is based on research that he conducted there.)[2] So, while Menninger's book drew attention to the disappearance of sin in our times, it was seed that fell on hard and rocky ground. It contained no careful psychological and cultural analysis of the new "self," a self for whom sin is a very foreign concept.

Instead, a cultural theorist, Christopher Lasch, drew the public's attention to the fact that this new self had indeed arrived on the scene. In 1979, Lasch's book *The Culture of Narcissism* was published, and it immediately became a best-seller.[3] In claiming that the narcissist is the dominant personality of our time, and exploring the psychological, sociological, and cultural implications of this claim, Lasch did not directly address Menninger's concern for whatever became of sin, but he noted the underlying threat to sin language in his preface: "The new narcissist is haunted not by guilt but by anxiety" (*CN*, 22). Whereas the pioneers of the pastoral counseling movement had linked guilt and anxiety, viewing anxiety as the psychological manifestation of the ontological

2. Otto Kernberg, *Borderline Conditions and Pathological Narcissism* (Northvale, N.J.: Jason Aronson, 1975).
3. Christopher Lasch, *The Culture of Narcissism: American Life in an Age of Diminishing Expectations* (New York: Warner Books, 1979).

condition of guilt, Lasch here separated guilt and anxiety, and claimed that the new self does not really experience guilt at all.

Now, the pioneers in the pastoral counseling movement might well argue that, because there is anxiety, there must also be guilt, and that the new narcissistic self is simply unaware of it. But this solution is much too facile; it fails to take account of the fact that the absence of guilt in the narcissistic self is quite real. Guilt has not simply been repressed. The axis around which the narcissistic self turns is not guilt but shame. What *was* repressed during the period that pastoral theology was so preoccupied with guilt—namely, the experience of shame—has now become manifest, and the truth of Erik Erikson's comment that shame "is an emotion insufficiently studied, because in our civilization it is so early and easily absorbed by guilt," is now being recognized.[4]

Lasch uses the term "new narcissist" in order to distinguish this emergent self from another self-type with which it might be confused, the "rugged individualist" of the late nineteenth and early twentieth centuries. While the "new narcissist" is similar to the "rugged individualist" in the sense that both are "isolates," "rugged individualists" are isolates by choice, normally because they consider the cause on which they are embarked to be too important for them to waste their time and energy in conviviality, small talk, and leisure pursuits. In contrast, the "new narcissists" are isolates because they cannot maintain interpersonal relationships, however desperately they try. One reason they so often fail in maintaining interpersonal relationships is that, unlike the rugged individualist, who *has* a cause, the new narcissist *is* his or her cause; when others discover this fact, they are sufficiently disillusioned or even disgusted that they take their leave.

But it is a serious mistake to lump the "individualist" and the "narcissist" together, as though they are identical. Such confounding of the two types of selves is a common practice in theological denunciations of both, and most unfortunate; it obscures the fact (as I will argue later) that narcissism is not, as is commonly

4. Erik H. Erikson, *Childhood and Society*, 2d rev. ed. (New York: W. W. Norton, 1963), 252.

believed, the effect of an individualism run amok, but of the diminishing influence of individualism in American institutional life, including our religious institutions.

To his credit, Lasch made a serious effort to engage the psychotherapeutic literature on narcissism, which enabled him to recognize substantial differences between the individualist and the narcissist. This difference is reflected in the subtitle of *The Culture of Narcissism: American Life in an Age of Diminishing Expectations*, and in the title of his subsequent book *The Minimal Self: Psychic Survival in Troubled Times*.[5] Whatever else might be said about nineteenth-century individualists, they did not view the age as one of diminishing opportunities, and they would have found it odd, and terribly sad, that a nation with such great human and natural resources would settle for something as minimalist as "psychic survival."

In giving serious attention to the writings of psychotherapists on narcissism, Lasch complains that much popular discussion of "narcissism" today is so loose and imprecise that it "retains little of its psychological content." For him, the value of consulting the clinical literature is that the more extreme, dysfunctional manifestations of narcissism, found in mental patients and other persons in therapy, tell us something about narcissism as a widespread social phenomenon. Furthermore, consideration of clinically inspired theories on narcissism enables one to identify the unique form that narcissism has taken in our own age. As he points out,

> Theoretical precision about narcissism is important not only because the idea is so readily susceptible to moralistic inflation but because the practice of equating narcissism with everything selfish and disagreeable mitigates against historical specificity. People have always been selfish, groups have always been ethnocentric; nothing is gained by giving these qualities a psychiatric label. The emergence of character disorders as the most prominent form of

5. Christopher Lasch, *The Minimal Self: Psychic Survival in Troubled Times* (New York: W. W. Norton, 1984).

psychiatric pathology, however, together with the change in personality structure this development reflects, derives from quite specific changes in our society and culture—from bureaucracy, the proliferation of images, therapeutic ideologies, the rationalization of the inner life, the cult of consumption, and . . . from changes in family life and . . . changing patterns of socialization. All of this disappears from sight if narcissism becomes simply "the metaphor of the human condition. . . ." (*CN*, 73–74)

One of the most significant features of Lasch's analysis is his view that narcissism, as a personality structure, goes hand in hand with bureaucracy, the type of social institution that predominates today.

For all his inner suffering, the narcissist has many traits that make for success in bureaucratic institutions, which put a premium on the manipulation of interpersonal relations, discourage the formation of deep personal attachments, and at the same time provide the narcissist with the approval he needs in order to validate his self-esteem. Although he may resort to therapies that promise to give meaning to life and to overcome his sense of emptiness, in his professional career the narcissist often enjoys considerable success. (*CN*, 91)

Since our churches have taken on many of the characteristics of bureaucracies, it is not surprising that clergy are sometimes rewarded, not punished, for their narcissistic behavior.

While Lasch makes use of clinical writings on narcissism, a weakness of his book is his selectivity in the use of that literature. While he provides a generally accurate picture of the narcissistic personality, he does not specifically identify those features of the narcissistic self that have the most critical bearing on our concerns here, namely, the disappearance of sin language and the need for its recovery. In the next chapter, therefore, I will take a more systematic look at the clinical literature on narcissism, much of which derives from the psychoanalytic tradition, which has had a particular investment in the tracking of this syndrome. That Jungian therapists have also been writing about the narcissistic self indicates that concern about narcissism is not limited to the Freudian tradition.[6]

6. See Nathan Schwartz-Salant, *Narcissism and Character Transformation* (Toronto: Inner City Books, 1982); and Mario Jacoby, *Individuation and Narcissism: The Psychology of Self in Jung and Kohut* (London: Routledge, 1990).

2

The
Narcissistic
Self

In the late 1950s and early 1960s, psychoanalysts, psychotherapists, and psychiatrists began to sense that a new type of patient was coming to them. The classical neurotic patient, beset by obsessive and compulsive behaviors attributable to a punitive superego, was being replaced by patients with characterological disorders. Initially viewed as antisocial personalities, suffering from a weak or nonexistent conscience, they were subsequently diagnosed as suffering instead from a weak or fragmentary self-structure that manifested itself in a variety of defensive maneuvers, the most notable being the resort to unrealistic self-inflation. This tendency toward self-inflated behavior and inappropriate assertions of personal grandiosity, which were incommensurate with actual ability or achievement, led the therapeutic community to conclude that this was the narcissistic personality. Freud had refused to treat this type, because he considered narcissists to be unanalyzable, owing to their presumed inability to form an emotional attachment to the therapist that could then be explored and interpreted.

Narcissistic Personality Disorder

Narcissism is generally considered the least severe of the "borderline conditions," which are a loose collection of characterological disorders that fall between neuroses on the one hand and psychoses on the other. Borderline disorders differ from neuroses primarily in that the former exhibit a poorly formed ego, a condition variously described as "identity diffusion," "self-fragmentation," "absence of clear ego boundaries," and the like. They differ, in turn, from psychoses, in that borderlines are clearly in touch with reality (i.e., they are not hallucinatory) and do not suffer the total disintegration of self that is typical, for example, of schizophrenia. Narcissism is considered the least severe borderline disorder because narcissists are able to function, often quite successfully, in the everyday world. They have greater control over their impulses to act in self-defeating ways, and are less likely to engage in the overtly self-destructive behaviors (such as attempted suicides) that are common among other borderlines.

Here is part of the official definition of the narcissistic personality disorder in the third edition of the *Diagnostic and Statistical Manual of Mental Disorders*, commonly called the DSM-III, Revised:[1]

> The essential feature of this disorder is a pervasive pattern of grandiosity (in fantasy or behavior), hypersensitivity to the evaluation of others, and lack of empathy that begins by early adulthood and is present in a variety of contexts.
>
> People with this disorder have a grandiose sense of self-importance. They tend to exaggerate their accomplishments and talents, and expect to be noticed as "special" even without appropriate achievement. They often feel that because of their "specialness," their problems are unique, and can be understood only by other special people. Frequently this sense of self-importance alternates

1. American Psychiatric Association, *Diagnostic and Statistical Manual of Mental Disorders*, 3d ed., revised (Washington, D.C.: American Psychiatric Association, 1987), 349–51. Copyright © 1987 American Psychiatric Association and reprinted by permission.

with feelings of special unworthiness. For example, a student who ordinarily expects an A and receives an A minus may, at that moment, express the view that he or she is thus revealed to all as a failure. Conversely, having gotten an A, the student may feel fraudulent, and unable to take genuine pleasure in a real achievement.

These people are preoccupied with fantasies of unlimited success, power, brilliance, beauty, or ideal love, and with chronic feelings of envy for those whom they perceive as being more successful than they are. Although these fantasies frequently substitute for realistic activity, when such goals are actually pursued, it is often with a driven, pleasureless quality and an ambition that cannot be satisfied.

Self-esteem is almost invariably very fragile; the person may be preoccupied with how well he or she is doing and how well he or she is regarded by others. This often takes the form of an almost exhibitionistic need for constant attention and admiration. The person may constantly fish for compliments, often with great charm. In response to criticism, he or she may react with rage, shame, or humiliation, but mask these feelings with an aura of cool indifference.

Interpersonal relationships are invariably disturbed. A lack of empathy (inability to recognize and experience how others feel) is common. For example, the person may be unable to understand why a friend whose father has just died does not want to go to a party. A sense of entitlement, an unreasonable expectation of especially favorable treatment, is usually present. For example, such a person may assume that he or she does not have to wait in line when others must. Interpersonal exploitativeness, in which others are taken advantage of in order to achieve one's ends, or for self-aggrandizement, is common. Friendships are often made only after the person considers how he or she can profit from them. In romantic relationships, the partner is often treated as an object to be used to bolster the person's self-esteem.

The DSM-III goes on to note that a depressed mood is extremely common, and it also observes that narcissistic personalities are often "painfully self-conscious and pre-occupied with grooming and remaining youthful" (DSM-III, 350). Underscoring its earlier point that narcissists tend to act in unprincipled ways, the DSM-III notes that "personal deficits, defeats, or irresponsible behavior may be justified by rationalization or lying. Feelings may be faked in order to impress others" (DSM-III, 350).

As far as the degree or extent of pathology is concerned, the DSM-III says that, of course, the narcissistic personality is impaired: "Some impairment in interpersonal relations is inevitable. Occupational functioning may be impeded by depressed mood, interpersonal difficulties, or the pursuit of unrealistic goals. In other cases, occupational functioning may be enhanced by an unquenchable thirst for success" (DSM-III, 350). Regarding the prevalence of the disorder, the DSM-III says that "this disorder appears to be more common recently than in the past, but this may be due only to more professional interest in it" (DSM-III, 350). Following Lasch's argument that the social conditions today are hospitable to the formation of narcissistic personalities, I do not think that one can account for the prevalence of this disorder solely on the grounds that professionals have greater interest in the disorder. Rather, such interest must certainly be a consequence of the fact that the disorder is more prevalent.

In short, the DSM-III offers a picture of the narcissistic personality as having an exaggerated or grandiose sense of self-importance; as having a remarkable absence of interest in and empathy for other persons; as eager to obtain admiration and approval from others; as entertaining fantasies of unrealistic goals; as lacking emotional depth, and unwilling or unable to understand the complex emotions of other people; as angry and resentful, but often concealing such resentment beneath depressive moods; as deficient in genuine feelings of sadness and compassion; as cold and indifferent, icy and unresponsive; as manipulative, exploitative, and unprincipled; as having strong feelings of insecurity and inferiority, alternating, but in no predictable pattern, with feelings of greatness and omnipotent fantasies; and as lacking enthusiasm and joy in the pursuit of goals, but reflecting, instead, a driven, pleasureless approach to goals, which are fueled by an insatiable ambition. Interpersonal relationships are extremely unstable due to a tendency either to overidealize or to devalue a relationship on an alternating basis. The other is expected to respond to one's desires and wants, but has no right to expect similar treatment in return.

Narcissism in Psychoanalytic Writings

The psychoanalytic movement has taken a particular interest in narcissism in recent years, owing in large part to the fact that the individuals coming to psychoanalysts for treatment have been more likely to manifest self disorders than the patients who were seen previously (who were more likely to be neurotics, i.e., obsessive-compulsives, sadomasochists, hypochondriacs, phobics, and the like).

Otto Kernberg, one of the leading psychoanalytic theorists on the narcissistic personality, describes the disorder in this way:

> On the surface, these patients may not present seriously disturbed behavior; some of them may function socially very well, and they usually have much better impulse control than the infantile personality.
>
> These patients present an unusual degree of self-reference in their interactions with other people, a great need to be loved and admired by others, and a curious apparent contradiction between a very inflated concept of themselves and an inordinate need for tribute from others. Their emotional life is shallow. They experience very little empathy for the feelings of others, they obtain very little enjoyment from life other than from the tributes they receive from others or from their grandiose fantasies, and they feel restless and bored when external glitter wears off and no new sources feed their self-regard. They envy others, tend to idealize some people from whom they expect narcissistic supplies and to depreciate and treat with contempt those from whom they do not expect anything (often their former idols). In general, their re-

lationships with other people are clearly exploitative and sometimes parasitic. It is as if they feel they have the right to control
and possess others and to exploit them without guilt feelings—
and, behind a surface which very often is charming and engaging,
one senses coldness and ruthlessness. Very often such patients are
considered to be dependent because they need so much tribute and
adoration from others, but on a deeper level they are completely
unable really to depend on anybody because of their deep distrust
and depreciation of others. (*BCPN*, 17)

From this description of the narcissistic personality, Kernberg
offers the following summary:

The main characteristic of these narcissistic personalities are grandiosity, extreme self-centeredness, and remarkable absence of interest and empathy for others in spite of the fact that they are so
very eager to obtain admiration and approval from other people.
These patients experience a remarkably intense envy of other
people who simply seem to enjoy their lives. These patients not
only lack emotional depth and fail to understand complex emotions
in other people, but their own feelings lack differentiation, with
quick flare-ups and subsequent dispersal of emotion. They are
especially deficient in genuine feelings of sadness and mournful
longing; their incapacity for experiencing depressive reactions is
a basic feature of their personalities. When abandoned or disappointed by other people they may show what on the surface looks
like depression, but which on further examination emerges as anger and resentment, loaded with revengeful wishes, rather than
real sadness for the loss of a person whom they appreciated.
(*BCPN*, 228–29)

Commenting on Kernberg's description of the narcissistic personality, Arnold Cooper notes that "the chief attributes described
in Kernberg's viewpoint are the individual's lack of emotional ties

to others, the lack of positive feelings about his own activities, and his inability to sustain relationships except as sources of admiration intended to bolster his own faltering self-esteem."[2] Another leading theorist, Heinz Kohut, also emphasizes the lack of genuine enthusiasm and joy, the sense of deadness and boredom, and the dependence on routines because the narcissist lacks initiative.[3] Along similar lines, Alexander Lowen makes special note of the narcissist's lack of or denial of feeling, the sense that one's body is without feeling, rigid, cold, and even dead, more like a mechanical object or machine than a living organism. While it is widely believed that narcissists are motivated to seek therapy when they tire of their inability to sustain a lasting relationship, Lowen believes that it is the fear of going insane that prompts most to seek therapy, a fear precipitated by their experience of their bodies as dead and lifeless, absent of feeling.[4]

Whether or not one agrees with Lowen's explanation for why narcissists seek therapy, it is clear that the narcissist is very much aware of his or her body, what it symbolizes and communicates, what it experiences or fails to experience, and what happens to it in the course of time. Recall that the original story of Narcissus, recounted in Ovid's *Metamorphoses*,[5] involved a young man who was physically very attractive, the object of Echo's passionate desire and longing, but was virtually devoid of any bodily feeling. Thus, the narcissistic disorder draws attention to the fact that the self is not a disembodied spirit, but is always embodied. The self is formed out of personality characteristics, social roles, and self-perceptions, but is always mediated in and

2. Arnold M. Cooper, "Narcissism," in Andrew P. Morrison, ed., *Essential Papers on Narcissism* (New York: New York Univ. Press, 1986), 130.
3. Heinz Kohut, *The Analysis of the Self: A Systematic Approach to the Psychoanalytic Treatment of Narcissistic Personality Disorders* (New York: International Universities Press, 1971), 16–17.
4. Alexander Lowen, *Narcissism: Denial of the True Self* (New York: Macmillan, 1983), 4ff.
5. Ovid, *Metamorphoses*, trans. A. D. Melville (New York: Oxford Univ. Press, 1987), 61–66.

through the body. The narcissist's self-structure is weak and fragmentary and lacking in boundaries because it is insecurely rooted in the body. For narcissists, the body is not a trustworthy monitor of feelings and perceptions, but is poorly attuned and unresponsive to the feelings and perceptions of other selves. In a word, it is nonempathic.

Another psychoanalytic theorist, Ben Bursten, suggests that narcissists may be distinguished from two other personality types, "complementary personalities" and "borderline personalities." Complementary personalities are able to achieve relationships in which one has a clear sense that the "other" fits in with one's own needs, and yet also "a sense of separateness from the other person which the narcissistic relationship lacks."[6] Thus, complementary personalities have a clear sense of the boundary between self and other, and are able to sustain relationships to others without loss of self. Borderlines, in Bursten's view, lack a clear sense of self, and are therefore always in danger of confusing the boundary between self and other. The borderline's sense of self is so fragile that self-fragmentation, or the disintegration of the self, is an ever-present danger.

For Bursten, the narcissist falls midway between the complementary personality and the borderline. In contrast to those who view the narcissist as the least pathological among the borderline types, Bursten sees the narcissist as not a borderline at all, for,

> in contrast to the borderline personality, the narcissistic personality has a firmer sense of self, feels (and is) in less danger of fragmenting, and has a better sense of reality testing. . . . While the narcissistic personalities have a firmer, more cohesive and stable ego organization than borderline personalities, they are not so able to separate themselves from others as are complementary personalities. This is seen, of course, in the narcissistic object choice—a reflection or extension of the narcissist himself, with little ability to respect the object as a person in his own right. (NPT, 381)

6. Ben Bursten, "Some Narcissistic Personality Types," in *EPN*, 380.

Because the borderline is in danger of self-fragmentation, whereas this is not a serious concern with the narcissist, one naturally tends to be less sympathetic toward the narcissist, to view the narcissist's lack of respect for the other less as a pathological condition and more as a fundamental character flaw. By distinguishing the narcissist from the borderline on the grounds that the narcissist is hardly in danger of self-loss, Bursten indirectly provides an explanation for why narcissists are the object of moral disapprobation.

Bursten also distinguishes the three types—borderline, narcissist, and complementary—in terms of what he calls "the task of the character structure." Thus, "the primary task of the complementary personality is to resolve the Oedipus complex—to combat the castration fear and overcome the guilt" (NPT, 381). In contrast, the task confronting the narcissistic personality is pre-Oedipal: "the main task of the narcissistic personality is to achieve the bliss and contentment characteristic of the primary narcissistic state, and this implies the reunion of the self which must be very grand with an object which must be nourishing and powerful" (NPT, 381). Thus, in comparison to the complementary personality, the narcissist's struggle is with more primitive issues, developmentally speaking. The complementary personality takes self-other relationships as givens, and as requiring negotiation and compromise, but the narcissist doubts the very existence of the self-other relationship. This, in turn, places one's self-esteem in jeopardy; "self-esteem, the approval of others, and the confirmation of one's sense of worth by the ability to use others are . . . derivatives of the earliest narcissistic state" (NPT, 381).

The task of the borderline personality is "to prevent disintegration and dissolution. It may seem to be related to the task of the narcissistic personality, for dissolution and psychic death is, in a sense, a return to the primary undifferentiated state. . . . [But] the borderline personality must struggle to prevent a regression towards the primary state itself while the narcissistic personality is governed by a need to satisfy the later derivatives of this primary state" (NPT, 382). Bursten acknowledges that the narcissistic personality may face the threat of disintegration when the narcissistic relationship is ruptured (i.e., when the "other," recognizing that he or she was not viewed or valued as an independent self, withdraws from the relationship), but narcissists "have a resilience which borderline personalities lack and they tend to 'snap back' and repair their narcissism" (NPT, 382). Thus, as far as the tasks of the character structure are concerned, the borderline's task is to prevent self-disintegration whereas the narcissist's task is to reunite with the other so as to regain critically needed emotional supplies. The narcissistic self is not in danger of falling apart, but is constantly concerned about becoming depleted, of being emotionally undernourished.

Narcissistic Personality Types

Bursten also offers a typology of narcissistic personalities, including the craving, paranoid, manipulative, and phallic types. This typology helps to account for and give some order to the diverse traits and characteristics of narcissists (revealed, for example, in the DSM-III description of the narcissistic personality). By identifying these types, Bursten shows that not all narcissists manifest all the traits that the DSM-III and other psychoanalysts ascribe to the narcissistic personality. Some narcissists reflect one cluster of traits, while others reflect different traits.

The *craving* personality reflects the tendency to be emotionally undernourished. This type includes many people who have been called "dependent" or "passive-aggressive"; indeed, "their interpersonal relationships are characterized by the need to have others support them. They are clingy, demanding, often pouting and whining. They act as though they constantly expect to be disappointed, and because of their extraordinary neediness, disappointment comes frequently. When not given to, they often seem to lack the energy to function, except for the function of increasing their demands in obvious or subtle ways" (NPT, 383).

In social situations, some craving personalities are quite charming and lively; yet, behind their charm is a certain desperation, and their liveliness has a driven quality. Other craving person-alities are less socially inclined; they cling to one person or to a very small group of people. The essential features of the craving personality are typically seen in their marriages, for, even in cases where they function adequately in their jobs, they collapse at home unless their spouses give them an inordinate amount of attention.

In Bursten's view, the terms "dependent" and "passive-aggressive" fail, in the final analysis, to grasp the essential fea-tures of this personality type. He doubts whether these individ-uals can really be dependent, for it is precisely because they cannot depend on anyone that they are so clinging. Nor is "passive-aggressive" an accurate term. It is usually employed by persons—therapists, work associates, spouses—who are trying to help the craving person become more independent and self-reliant. The tendency of such personalities to resist these efforts are deemed to be passive-aggressive, i.e., a subtle ploy on the part of the craving personality to undermine efforts of others to help them overcome their dependency. But craving individuals are not trying to wean themselves from dependency; rather, they are desperately seeking dependence, and therefore they simply do not identify with the goal of freeing them from their "de-pendencies." When they resist such goals, they are not being passive-aggressive but demonstrating that, for them, such efforts are counterproductive.

The better term, therefore, is the "craving personality," which one of Bursten's own patients suggested to him when he corrected Bursten's references to his constant state of neediness: "Needi-ness," he said, "it isn't just neediness. It's craving. I'm like a little bird with a wide-open beak" (NPT, 384). Craving personalities, then, are characterized by the very fact of their neediness. Com-plementary personalities *have* specific needs that they identify and then seek to have met; the craving type of narcissistic per-sonality *is* needy. One may attempt to identify the craving person's needs and then devise ways in which these needs may be met, but this misses the point: the neediness of the craving personality cannot be met by the meeting of specific needs. The neediness is deeply rooted in the self, and reflects a void that no amount of need-satisfactions can fill. This is why the craving of this type seems insatiable, why the hunger for emotional nourishment is like a bottomless pit, and why the cry for more is such an insistent, demanding refrain.

The *paranoid* type of narcissist is, in Bursten's view, well described by the DSM-III: "This behavioral pattern is characterized by hypersensitivity, rigidity, unwarranted suspicion, jealousy, envy, excessive self-importance, and a tendency to blame others and ascribe evil motives to them" (NPT, 384). Bursten emphasizes that these paranoid types lead active and productive lives, especially in vocations where skepticism, suspiciousness, and criticism are important components. Often they are litigious and generally argumentative. Their anger runs the gamut from faultfinding and complaining to jealous rages.

The term "paranoid" is an appropriate description because this narcissistic personality type projects self-contempt onto others. Unable to endure the contempt they have for themselves, they project it outward, and direct their criticisms and suspicions toward other persons, often toward their spouses. Unable to love themselves, they assume that the other is feigning love for them or is secretly cheating on them. An innocent friendship enjoyed by the spouse sends the paranoid type into a jealous rage. The paranoid type therefore reflects what is true of all the narcissistic personality types, for while narcissists are popularly viewed as being in love with themselves, they are in fact engulfed in self-hatred. The paranoid's self-contempt is so great that the genuine love that another may feel for him or her is viewed with great suspicion, and this suspiciousness, in turn, drives the other away, thus seeming to confirm the truth of the paranoid personality's allegations.

The *manipulative* type of narcissistic personality is usually discussed in clinical literature under the rubric of the "antisocial personality," but Bursten finds this as questionable as the tendency to refer to craving types as "passive-aggressive." He considers the current designations of the antisocial or sociopathic personality misleading because they rely on a combination of psychological and sociological criteria. Too often the diagnosis is made on the basis of a record of repeated offenses and conflicts with the law. For him, the issue is manipulation, which may just as well occur in the context of socially approved as in socially disapproved activities. Manipulation, like craving, is an intra-psychic phenomenon, and thus independent of whether the manipulation actually succeeds: "The manipulator perceives that another person's goal conflicts with his own, he intends to influence the other person and employs deception in the influencing process, and he has the satisfying feeling of having put something over on the other person when the manipulation works" (NPT, 385). This is a conscious, not unconscious, process, as the manipulator is fully aware of what he or she is doing. Typically, the act of "putting something over" on the other is carefully planned and executed, often by first eliciting the other person's trust and then exploiting this trust. When the manipulation succeeds, the manipulator typically expresses disdain for the other; the other was "gullible," "naive," or a "pushover," and thus not tough enough to survive in the dog-eat-dog world of today. Thus the manipulator views unprincipled behavior as justified, and it is the trusting victim, not oneself, whose character is severely flawed.

The manipulative personality is characterized by lying, little apparent guilt, transient and superficial relationships, and considerable contempt for other people. Manipulative types seem not to learn from experience; they persist in manipulative behavior even after these efforts have been rebuffed or successfully counteracted by their intended victims. The failure to learn from experience is due to the fact that the manipulative personality has an inner compulsion to manipulate, which exists independently of the rewards that accrue from manipulative behavior. As craving personalities crave, and paranoid personalities suspect, so manipulative personalities manipulate. It is not a matter of manipulating until one has what one wants, and then ceasing to manipulate, for manipulation is what one is, and is therefore self-defining. The charge, "He or she is a real manipulator," puts it very well. Where the craving personality demands, whines, and pouts in an effort to gain emotional supplies, the manipulative personality gets what he or she desires by means of deceit, lies, and deviousness.

The *phallic* type of narcissist is most often male, and is characterized by the need to parade his masculinity, often along athletic or aggressive lines: "In common with some manipulative personalities, they tend to be both exhibitionist and reckless. While the exhibitionism of the manipulative personality tends more to call attention to his 'good behavior' and reputation, the phallic narcissist tends more to show himself off and to exhibit his body, clothes, and manliness. The manipulative person is more reckless in his schemes, deceptions and manipulations; the phallic narcissist tends more towards feats of reckless daring, such as driving automobiles at excessive speeds, in order to prove his power" (NPT, 385). Arrogance is the major feature of phallic narcissism.

Male phallic narcissists have a dual attitude toward women. On the one hand, they talk about women in the contemptuous terms of locker-room language; on the other hand, they are the defenders of motherhood and the sanctity of women. Female phallic narcissists are far less common; like their male counterparts, they often are very conscious of their clothes and cars, and tend to be arrogant, cold, and haughty.

An especially noteworthy feature of phallic narcissism is that the body becomes an instrument for acquiring attention, admiration, and influence over others. As it was Narcissus's physical attractiveness that held Echo in thrall, the phallic type is the one popularly associated with narcissism, and is largely responsible for the view that narcissists are so much in love with themselves that they are not only unable to love others, but also seem to take sadistic pleasure in refusing to let their admirers get too close. While the inability to sustain a lasting relationship is characteristic of narcissists, and while the phallic narcissist's failure in this regard appears to be due largely to his or her excessive self-love, the truth is that the phallic narcissist is just like all other narcissists, i.e., profoundly lacking in self-love. Phallic narcissism, then, is an attempt, futile and vain as it may be, to overcome a pervasive sense of self-contempt, of shame for who and what one is, by acting in an arrogant and conceited manner. Like the craving personality, phallic narcissists are emotionally starved; but, unlike the craving personality, phallic narcissists pretend that they are everything that they could possibly need.

Modes of Narcissistic Repair

Having identified these four narcissistic types, Bursten describes how each of them goes about the task of narcissistic repair. Narcissistic repair has to do with the individual's efforts to restore the self-esteem that was experienced in the early months of infancy (the period of "primary narcissism"). Since such self-esteem has proven so vulnerable and tenuous, repair is typically a lifelong project. The mode of repair differs for each of the four types.

For the *craving* type, repair involves opening the beak even wider: "The craving personality must be fed. He is devastated if supplies and nourishment are not forthcoming. . . . While he is unfed, his self-esteem suffers; where is his specialness and where are the nourishing objects?" (NPT, 387). Such efforts to regain resources of nourishment often have an aggressive feature, emanating from anger over their withdrawal or absence; such aggression typically takes the form of pouting and sulking. One may even reject the nourishment that is offered so as to pout and sulk a little longer. Or one may accept the proffered nourishment but express hurt that one had to beg for it; the other did not instinctively realize what was needed and provide it without having to be asked.

The sulking and complaining of the craving personality takes on a much more hostile tone in the *paranoid* personality, whose mode of repair is expressed through argumentativeness, jealousy, and critical suspiciousness. The paranoid personality feels betrayed, and much of the critical attitude of this type of person says, "Why does someone else get things and I don't?" Thus, the complaints of paranoid personalities portray the need to be the special, selected ones, and they hope that, by complaining of the ill-treatment they have received, they will regain the special relationship with the other that they previously enjoyed. Yet, since these complaints are tinged with criticism, suspicion, and argumentativeness, they often have the opposite effect—they drive the other away. As noted earlier, the criticism and suspiciousness that the paranoid narcissist directs toward the other is a projection of shameful self-feelings, a way of trying to get rid of them by shaming the other instead: "Thus he is critical, argumentative, suspicious, and he constantly looks for signs of shameful conduct in others, both as a public repudiation of his own inner feelings and as external affirmation and support of his projections" (NPT, 391).

The mode of repair of the *manipulative* personality is successfully "putting something over" on another person. When the manipulation succeeds, it purges the shameful, worthless self-image, which is attributed instead to the victim. Exhilaration results; the newly "cleansed" self is now glorified and powerful. Shame has temporarily given way to grandiosity; one is, at least for the time being, thoroughly pleased with what one has achieved, and oblivious, of course, to the future consequences of one's glorious triumph.

Where the craving, paranoid, and manipulative types seek to overcome disrepair through behavior that makes a direct appeal or demand on another, the *phallic* personality goes about repair not by direct pursuit of supplies from others, but by relying on fantasized expectations of others' admiration and adulation. Repair involves counteracting the shame of being weak through the creation of a self-image of virility, power, and physical attractiveness. It takes the form of arrogance, self-glorification, aggressive competitiveness, and pseudomasculinity, which is often demonstrated in foolish acts of bravery. Craving personalities tend to deplete the other, using up the other's emotional supplies; phallic personalities seek the other's admiration, exploiting the other's own narcissistic cravings. Unlike the manipulative personality, who exploits the other's trust, the phallic personality exploits the other's need to idealize another, to bask in another's glow. Thus, of the four types, only the phallic type takes advantage of the deep narcissistic needs of others—their own longing to be admired and loved—and then cruelly denies the other because he or she is emotionally incapable of meeting these needs. Like Echo, the other is eventually depleted, drained of emotion, and thus drained of life itself.

Bursten's accounts of how the four types go about narcissistic repair indicate that, in all four cases, the repairs are symptomatic of their pathologies. In each case, the repair takes the form of doing *more* of what they had been doing, even though this was what got them into their current state of vulnerability. Thus, the craving personality craves more, the paranoid personality becomes even more suspicious, the manipulative personality manipulates more, and the phallic personality engages in greater self-promotion. Narcissists' own efforts to repair the damage are therefore counterproductive, and they reveal that a more forceful effort to acquire what is felt to be lacking in their lives is no real solution to the problem.[7]

Developmental Roots of Narcissism

A major concern of psychoanalytic (or Freudian) theorists has been to account for the emergence of the narcissistic personality type, and this attempt has produced a great deal of theorizing about what must have happened to these individuals in infancy or early childhood. The consensus is that this disorder is rooted in pre-Oedipal experience (i.e., before the age of three), and that

7. See, on this point, Paul Watzlawick, John Weakland, and Richard Fisch, *Change: Principles of Problem Formation and Problem Resolution* (New York: W. W. Norton, 1974). Here, the authors distinguish between first-order change, or situations in which change results in everything remaining much as it was before, and second-order change, where the situation is fundamentally changed (i.e., there is change in change itself). I have discussed this distinction in my *Reframing: A New Method in Pastoral Care* (Minneapolis: Fortress Press, 1990), 12–13.

it has much to do with the "separation and individuation" stage (between ages one and three). In terms of Erik Erikson's life-cycle theory, it corresponds to the second stage, "autonomy vs. shame and doubt." While we cannot delve into the complexities of these efforts to trace narcissism developmentally, much less try to adjudicate the controversies they have spawned among the various theorists, we can sketch a general picture of what is claimed to be happening in this early period of life.

Theorists like Heinz Kohut suggest that the infant comes into the world with a narcissism that is entirely healthy. Infants experience themselves as the center of the universe, and everything around them is perceived as an extension of themselves. They are their world, and their world is them. But, in time, they become aware of the fact that the world "out there" has its own independent existence, and with this discovery, they have their first experience of "narcissistic injury." The world, they begin to sense, does not exist solely for them, and they are not, in fact, the very center of all that is. The realization of these facts is a powerful assault on the infant's basic narcissism, and leads to a defensive reaction commonly called "splitting." Kohut's analysis of this splitting process and its effects is rather complex, but one feature of the process that explains some of the inherent contradictions in the narcissistic personality is the emergence of two self parts: a grandiose self (given to exaggerated self-importance) and a depleted self (given to feelings of shame, humiliation, and worthlessness) (*RS*, 171–219). The grandiose self is a defense against the deflating experience of discovering that one is not, after all, the center of reality, while the depleted or shameful self is an exaggerated response to narcissistic injury, an overreaction to the blow that one has sustained to what was perfectly healthy narcissism.

Kohut calls this defensive response "secondary narcissism," and says that no one, even those whose early years were spent in ideal conditions, has been able to avoid it (*RS*, 63–129). "Secondary narcissism" is more severe among those who have suffered great narcissistic injury, normally due to inadequate parental attention and affection during the separation-individuation stage.

As Kohut and others have noted, narcissistic personalities are likely to have been emotionally *under*stimulated during infancy, often due to the fact that their parents were themselves cold, aloof, or even indifferent, lacking in empathy, and thus unable or unwilling to mirror the child's desire to be loved and to love in return.

Our need for mirroring, a key theme in Kohut's work, concerns the actual and symbolic role of the adult's face in the forming of the infant's emotional life. When the adult returns the infant's smile, the infant experiences self-recognition, which is inherently pleasurable, and learns that his or her own behavior can evoke a positive, loving response from another. If, on the other hand, the adult is an unreliable mirror, whether by failing to return the child's smile, or returning it only on some but not all occasions, the infant experiences rejection, and insecurity and self-mistrust follow. Parents' failure to mirror the infant is often due to their own emotional depletion. Our lifelong need for adequate mirroring will be a recurring theme throughout this book (*RS*, 115–18).

The same splitting that occurs within the emerging self also occurs in self-other relationships. Infants who have had to accept the truth that they are not the very center of the world, and are therefore unlikely to be able to exercise absolute control over events of great importance to themselves—to their very survival—will begin to idealize those, especially the mothering person, who are responsible for their well-being. This person must be idealized, for otherwise the infant will be overcome with fears of abandonment, of being faced with the impossible task of surviving on one's own. Parents who are inwardly secure, who have a healthy narcissism themselves, will not be put off by their child's idealization of them, but will play along with it, recognizing that it serves a vital role in enabling the child to feel secure and protected. Conversely, parents who are bored, embarrassed, or even disgusted by such idealization will withdraw, leaving the child confused, despairing, and further depleted. Such parents fail to realize how much the child's own sense of self depends on this idealization of parents being mirrored back to the child. In their essay on the disorders of the self, Kohut and Wolf offer the following illustration:

> A little boy is eager to idealize his father, he wants his father to tell him about his life, the battles he engaged in and won. But instead of joyfully acting in accordance with his son's need, the father is embarrassed by the request. He feels tired and bored and, leaving the house, finds a temporary source of vitality for his enfeebled self in the tavern, through drink and mutually supportive talk with friends.[8]

In addition to idealizations of others that are internalized as self-idealizations, secondary narcissism gives rise to personal ambitions. If I am not in fact the center of the world, then I must strive to be what I, by nature, am not. Here again, the parents are of crucial importance: they validate the child's ambitions through interest and encouragement, and invalidate them through their lack of interest. Kohut and Wolf present the following illustration: "A little girl comes home from school, eager to tell her mother about some great success. But the mother, instead of listening with pride, deflects the conversation from the child to herself, [and] begins to talk about her own successes which overshadow those of her little daughter" (DSTT, 184). Here the parent's mirroring of the child's ambitions is lacking. The child's search for an expression of pride on the mother's face, which would confirm the child's own inner glow, is instead deflected. In contrast to the first illustration, here the child's desire was that she herself be prized. In effect, good parenting involves the capacity of the adult to mirror the child's emotions and perceptions, to validate them as appropriate and true. The absence of mirroring leads to self-depletion, to the formation of a very insecure, undernourished self. If St. Paul can endure seeing in a mirror dimly, this is because he can anticipate that, one day, he will see God face-to-face (1 Cor. 13:12). But the child who has

8. Heinz Kohut and Ernest S. Wolf, "The Disorders of the Self and Their Treatment: An Outline," in *EPN*, 184.

experienced no validation of his or her ideals and ambitions has nothing but an opaque mirror. Without mirroring, there can be no self; the light of the self depends on the mirroring it receives from without.

In one of his most beautiful, poignant images, Kohut tells the familiar story of the child who runs from her mother for the first time, then, overwhelmed with anxiety and doubt, turns around, searching her mother's face for indications of how she views this radically new development. The mother, herself unthreatened by this turn of events, smiles encouragingly, and the child smiles in return, and runs a little farther. This, Kohut suggests, is how children grow into selves that are confident, assured, and inwardly happy.[9]

In emphasizing the Oedipus complex, Freud entertained a scenario in which the child has unacceptable desires and feelings toward parental figures, and experiences relations with others as deeply conflictual and openly hostile. For Kohut and others who emphasize the decisiveness of pre-Oedipal experience, the problem is more basic than this. At issue is the very formation of the self, the problem of actually becoming a coherent self that, as Kohut and Wolf express it, is "an independent center of initiative, an independent recipient of impressions" (DSTT, 178). For those who are struggling to become a self, actual conflicts with others, such as those encountered in the Oedipal stage, are often conspicuous by their absence, or relatively unimportant. Certainly they do not assume the decisive role in the child's development that Freud ascribed to them, for such conflicts assume that the child has a self that is sufficiently strong that it may risk itself in conflict or negotiation with others. Compromise is possible because one knows that such compromise will not be self-annihilating. For Freud, neurotic structures result from conflicts with parental figures that are inadequately worked through. For Kohut, the primary pathologies of our time are self pathologies, resulting from inadequately formed or poorly established selves.

9. Heinz Kohut, *How Does Analysis Cure?* (Chicago: Univ. of Chicago Press, 1984), 187–88.

The Hungry Self

Kohut and Wolf use the metaphor of hunger to characterize those who suffer from such self pathologies (DSTT, 189–92). Such persons experience themselves as suffering from inner depletion. For Kohut and Wolf, such hunger may take a number of different forms. The *mirror-hungry* personalities "thirst for self-objects whose confirming and admiring responses will nourish their famished self." The *ideal-hungry* personalities "are forever in search of others whom they can admire for their prestige, power, beauty, intelligence, or moral stature. They can experience themselves as worthwhile only so long as they can relate to self-objects to whom they can look up." The *alter-ego-hungry* personalities "need a relationship with a self-object that by conforming to the self's appearance, opinions, and values confirms the existence, the reality of the self." Except in rare instances, however, the inner void of the self cannot be filled permanently by this twinship of self and other. The alter-ego-hungry personality discovers that the other is not oneself and, as a consequence of this discovery, begins to feel estranged from the other: "It is thus characteristic for most of these relationships to be short-lived. Like the mirror- and ideal-hungry, the alter-ego hungry is prone to look restlessly for one replacement after another" (DSTT, 190–91).

Kohut and Wolf emphasize that these three character types in the narcissistic realm "are frequently encountered in everyday life and they should, in general, not be considered as forms of psychopathology but rather as variants of the normal human personality, with its assets and defects." More pathological than mirror-hungry, ideal-hungry, and alter-ego-hungry selves are *merger-hungry* personalities, whose behavior is "dominated by the fact that the fluidity of the boundaries between them and others interferes with their ability to discriminate their own thoughts, wishes and intentions from those of the self object," and *contact-shunning* personalities, who "avoid social contact and become isolated, not because they are disinterested in others, but, on the contrary, just because their need for them is so intense." Hunger-language also applies in the case of these more

Andrew Morrison

severely pathological types of narcissistic selves. Merger-hungry persons are like Pac-Man, cannibalizing others,[10] while contact-shunning personalities are apprehensive "that the remnants of their nuclear self will be *swallowed up* [my emphasis] and destroyed by the yearned-for all-encompassing union" (DSTT, 192). Given these descriptions of narcissistic personality types as hungry, empty, or in danger of being swallowed, it is not surprising that one of the more prominent pathologies of our times is the eating disorder, whose psychodynamic roots are explored by Kim Chernin in *The Hungry Self*.[11] It is as though the eating disorder is a metaphor for our times in much the same way that demon-possession was in Jesus' time.[12] If demon possession is the sense that one is inhabited by an alien power (even as Israel itself was so inhabited), the eating disorder is symptomatic and symbolic of the inner depletion characteristic of the narcissistic self.

The Shameful Self

Another prevalent theme in the literature on narcissism is the shameful self. In contrast to Freud, who emphasized the guilt feelings that result from unacceptable desires felt toward parental objects, Kohut stresses the shameful feelings that result from poor parental mirroring of ideals and ambitions. Kohut calls Freud's Oedipal personality the Guilty Self, and refers to the pre-Oedipal, narcissistic personality as the Tragic Self (*RS*, 206–7, 224–25). The Tragic Self knows very little guilt, but is well acquainted with feelings of deep shame, which are immobilizing and debilitating.

In "Shame, Ideal Self, and Narcissism," Andrew Morrison notes that "shame has been relegated to second-order importance

10. Richard K. Fenn, *The Secularization of Sin: An Investigation of the Daedalus Complex* (Louisville: Westminster/John Knox Press, 1991).
11. Kim Chernin, *The Hungry Self: Women, Eating and Identity* (New York: Harper & Row, 1985).
12. See Paul W. Hollenbach, "Jesus, Demoniacs, and Public Authorities: A Socio-Historical Study," *Journal of the American Academy of Religion* 49, no. 4 (1981): 567–88.

in classic psychoanalytic literature" because it relates directly to the self—a construct that until recently "has not been easily integrated into the mainstream of Freudian concepts. . . ."[13] Instead, shame "is about the whole self, and its failure to live up to an ideal; as such, it is a 'narcissistic' reaction. A typical defense against shame is hiding, or running away. Hostility against self is experienced in a passive mode, and therefore leaves the shame-prone individual subject to depression. Guilt, on the other hand, refers to a transgression, an action, and therefore has a more specific cognitive or behavioral antecedent than shame, referring less globally to the subjective sense of self."[14] Morrison concludes that "the referent of shame, then, is the self, which is experienced as defective, inadequate, and having failed in its quest to attain a goal" (*EPN*, 351). Whereas guilt arises in experience from failing to meet the expectations, real or perceived, of others, shame is felt when the self has failed to attain its own goals, when the realization occurs that the self is incapable of achieving its ambitions. The person who is hurt or damaged by this assessment is not another person, but the self. The typical effects of such overwhelming shame are depletion, hollowness, and unfulfilled hunger.

The hungry self (Kohut) and the shameful self (Morrison) have similar psychodynamic roots, reflecting the self's experience of depletion and devaluation, its sense of being irreparably damaged through no fault of its own. Note that the narcissistic personality neither claims to be without guilt nor is beyond committing certain wrongful acts that can hurt and damage other persons. Guilt and the desire to be free of guilt are not, however, the driving force of the narcissistic personality. Narcissists are painfully aware that something is wrong with them. This awareness, however, is not

13. Andrew P. Morrison, "Shame, Ideal Self, and Narcissism," in *EPN*, 348. See also idem, *Shame: The Underside of Narcissism* (Hillsdale, N. J.: Analytic Press, 1989).
14. See *EPN*, 350; Morrison refers to Helen Block Lewis, *Shame and Guilt in Neurosis* (New York: International Universities Press, 1971), 35–40.

based on the traditional psychoanalytic view that the sense of being culpable is rooted in the interpersonal conflict between child and parents, as the illicit, antisocial desires of the child are opposed by parents whose task is to confront these desires and to help the child redirect them in socially constructive ways.

Because this traditional psychoanalytic view has affinities with the Christian view of guilt—both assume that the natural will needs to be conformed to the will of another who knows what is good for us—Christian theology is faced with a problem similar to the one psychoanalysis confronted in the 1950s and 1960s: having, on the one hand, a perfectly good theory of what is wrong with us and what therefore needs to happen in order for us to be set right, but having, on the other hand, a constituency whose life experience is not significantly related to the theory. Psychoanalysis had answers to the problems of the few, while the problems of the many, soon to become the vast majority, remained outside the theory. In the same way, Christian theology has well-developed theologies of guilt, while the majority of its constituency is struggling with the debilitating, demoralizing, and even dehumanizing effects of shame. So far, the church has dealt with this issue in rather superficial ways, usually by engaging in moralistic condemnation of the narcissistic personality of our times.

Yet, in contrast to the self-image narcissists seek to project, they are profoundly unhappy and dissatisfied with their lives and with themselves. Seeming to be self-loving and self-satisfied, they instead have a deep sense of personal shame and self-contempt. One should still hold narcissists responsible for their behavior, especially where it is unprincipled, deceitful, exploitative, and abusive. But clinical studies of narcissism have shown that narcissists have also been the victims of emotional deprivations that are most certainly undeserved.

To speak of narcissists as "them" is, however, misleading. Even though an individual may not be a narcissistic personality in the clinical sense of the term, clinical pathologies of a society in a given era are reflective, however exaggeratedly and distortedly, of the general society.[15] Bureaucratic structures cause many to feel unappreciated and devalued as we search in vain for a face that takes notice and affirms our value and worth. Our consumer-oriented culture causes us to view the exterior world as a panorama of objects that are either disposable or constantly being devalued. Is it any wonder that we experience ourselves and other persons as no less transient and no less subject to devaluation?

Narcissism has its highly manipulative and exhibitionistic side, epitomized by the machinations and life-styles of "the rich and famous." In our own ways and in our own settings and contexts of work and family life, we have been known to employ the meaner, less flamboyant methods of the craving, paranoid, manipulative, and phallic narcissists: sulking and pouting, criticizing and suspecting, deceiving and exploiting, showing off and putting down. Even when we are not engaged in such questionable methods of self-repair, we seem chronically depleted, doubtful of our worth, emotionally hungry, and highly attuned and sensitive to shame. Moments of elation and satisfaction cannot be enjoyed or even trusted because we know that soon the bubble will burst, the joy will dissipate, and the life will go out of us, leaving us, once again, feeling empty and depleted.

If the narcissistic self is so beset by shame, we need to resist moralistic condemnations and view narcissism more sympathetically. In this regard, the theological community has not been very helpful, as it has either encouraged the moralistic condemnation of narcissism or responded with insights relevant to an earlier era. Conceivably this narcissistic era will soon pass, as some of our social prognosticators are already suggesting. If so, Christian theology might consider riding out the storm until conditions return to what they were before the age of narcissism. But I doubt that this era of the narcissistic self will pass anytime soon, as there is no evidence to suggest that the social structures that support it (bureaucracy in the workplace and consumerism

15. For Kohut's views, see *The Restoration of the Self* (New York: International Universities Press, 1977), 277ff.

in the marketplace) are in any danger of collapse. Rather, they are becoming more entrenched than ever. Our religious institutions reflect these social trends, and are therefore less effective as a counterforce against the narcissism that their leaders have been so quick to condemn. The very idea that Christian theology might ride out the storm must also be anathema to a people whose Lord did not merely talk about the hungry, but went about feeding them.

3

The Deadliest Sins of Our Narcissistic Age

The declining importance of sin language today is related to the emergence of the narcissistic personality. Because sin has been so intimately associated with guilt in Christian consciousness, and because traditional Christian theology has been concerned to provide support for this association of sin and guilt, sin has become an irrelevant, or, at least, a devalued concept. Clinical writings attest that the narcissist does not experience guilt to any significant degree.

Even though narcissists are not as burdened with neurotic guilt, they nonetheless do not feel whole, healthy, or happy. Were they to feel healthy, then the moralistic indictments of narcissism would be entirely appropriate and justified. But narcissists are burdened, among other things, with a deep, chronic, and often inexplicable sense of shame. Shame has replaced guilt as the experience that causes individuals to feel bad about themselves, to feel that something is seriously wrong with them. They may not use religious language to describe it or be fully aware that through their sense of shame they are experiencing humanity's sinful nature. But, if such awareness is to emerge, then it will result from their struggle to understand their shameful self, with its sense of inner depletedness and of unmet hunger for admiration and approval, and for positive mirroring of their need to idealize self and others. Such awareness will not emerge, however, by acceding to pronouncements that they are guilty for sins not committed or actions for which no guilt is felt.

Admittedly, the clinical literature focuses on pathological forms of narcissism, on persons whose symptoms are more severe or chronic than the normal population. Does it exaggerate the painful side of narcissism as far as the general population is concerned? Might it not be the case that only those who are seriously ill experience the painful features of the narcissistic syndrome—the shameful self—while those who are normal experience only its self-aggrandizing features, the grandiose self, with which we normally associate the word "narcissism"? Or might it even be the case that normal persons, unlike the clinically diagnosed narcissists, are not struggling with narcissistic issues at all, whether grandiosity, shame, or some combination of the two?

There is also the question of whether narcissism, in whatever form, is more characteristic of certain age groups and social classes in American society than of others, thus justifying the tendency of certain groups to indict other groups, usually for self-aggrandizing, not shame-related, behavior. For example, older adults often indict young professionals for their narcissistic attitudes and life-styles, whereas post-retirement adults are rarely so indicted, even though their attitudes and life-styles may be similar to those of the young professional classes. A related question that especially concerns those in Christian ministry is whether church members differ from the general population as far as narcissism is concerned. Are practicing Christians any less narcissistic than the general population?

Questions of this nature cannot be answered on theoretical grounds alone. They require empirical research, and yet there has been no systematic effort to study narcissism among practicing Christians. This lack is significant in itself; it suggests that narcissism is one of those many phenomena that we moralize about largely on the basis of impressions and hearsay. To correct this lack, in 1988 I conducted a study of committed laity that has direct bearing on the narcissism question, and in 1989 I repeated the same study with a clergy population.[1] Much of this chapter reports the findings of this study, which make a persuasive case for the view that narcissism is not limited to specific age groups. Furthermore, the study provides evidence that Christian laity and clergy are struggling with the painful features of the narcissistic syndrome. This latter claim is especially interesting; it suggests that Christian laity and clergy are suffering, in deep and pervasive ways, from the narcissistic syndrome of our times, and that their sense of dis-ease, unwholeness, and unhappiness is on a continuum with clinical narcissism. This study also reveals that Christian laity and clergy have conceptions of sin that are generally congruent with a theology of guilt, whereas their actual experience of sinfulness—of a deep inner sense of wrongness—is more reflective of the psychodynamics of shame.

The "Deadly Sins" Formula

The empirical study grew out of my earlier proposals for relating the traditional deadly sins formula to the stages of the life cycle as developed by Erik and Joan Erikson.[2] The traditional deadly sins system can be traced, historically, to the fourth century, and, more specifically, to the Egyptian monk Evagrius of Pontus, who formulated a list of eight deadly sins. His protégé, John of Cassian, who set the standards for Western monasticism that were influential throughout the Middle Ages, preserved the eight deadly sins formula. For him, they were gluttony, lust,

1. See Donald Capps, "The Deadly Sins and Saving Virtues: How They Are Viewed by Laity," in *Pastoral Psychology* 37, no. 4 (1989): 229–53; "The Deadly Sins and Saving Virtues: How They Are Viewed by Clergy," in *Pastoral Psychology* 40, no. 4 (1992): 209–33. Also relevant is my article, "Sin, Narcissism, and the Changing Face of Conversion," in *Journal of Religion and Health* 29 (1990): 233–51.
2. Erik H. Erikson, *CS*, 247–74. Joan M. Erikson, *Wisdom and the Senses: The Way of Creativity* (New York: W. W. Norton, 1988), 74–112.

covetousness, anger, dejection, boredom, vanity, and pride. According to William E. Paden, "Cassian explained the causes and cures for each. Without the skills to combat them, the monk would become 'subject' to these vices. Applying the skills, the vices would become subject to the monk's determination." Paden also observes that "Cassian's vocabulary highlights the active, determinative character of this system. There is consistent use of terms for struggling, resisting, overcoming, fighting, prevailing. He relies on words for attaining, achieving, gaining, winning, victory. His writings are saturated with the language of vigilance, discrimination, watching, weighing."[3]

Those familiar with the "seven deadly sins" formula will, of course, be surprised to learn that the original lists consisted of eight deadly sins. It was not until the sixth century that efforts were made to pare the list from eight to seven, possibly to have one deadly sin for each day of the week, enabling one to concentrate each day on the sin assigned to it.[4] Since there was never an official list of eight sins, this reduction was not simply a matter of eliminating the least deadly sin from an already established list. Two sins were the focus of considerable discussion and debate. These were *acedia*, or apathy, which Cassian captured in his sin of boredom, and *tristitia*, or melancholy, which is more or less covered by Cassian's sin of dejection. In reducing the list from eight to seven, Pope Gregory the Great subsumed apathy under melancholy, while the theologian Alcuin did the reverse, incorporating melancholy into apathy. In the course of time, Alcuin's proposal prevailed, and melancholy was no longer viewed as one of the deadly sins, though it continued to be viewed as one form or expression of apathy. "Sloth" is the word used for

3. William E. Paden, "Theaters of Humility and Suspicion: Desert Saints and New England Puritans," in Luther H. Martin, Huck Gutman, and Patrick H. Hutton, eds., *Technologies of the Self: A Seminar with Michel Foucault* (Amherst, Mass.: Univ. of Massachusetts Press, 1988), 66.

4. See my argument in this regard in *Deadly Sins and Saving Virtues* (Philadelphia: Fortress Press, 1987), 12.

this sin in the ancient rule of the Anchorites, and by Chaucer in "The Parson's Tale" in *Canterbury Tales*.[5]

While the word "apathy" may retain elements of melancholy, it is doubtful that the word "sloth" has significant melancholic connotations (dejection, depression, discouragement, bitterness, and the like). So, when sloth became the name for this sin, traces of melancholy began to disappear from the official formula. Over the past few centuries, a further erosion has occurred, for certainly the understanding of "sloth" today has few of the apathetic connotations it had centuries ago, when sloth meant not only inactivity and idleness, but also a lifeless and heavy heart, and a despairing attitude reflected in a refusal of God's mercy and grace.

Whether vanity or vainglory should be viewed as a deadly sin in its own right, or subsumed under the sin of pride, was also debated. Some lists, such as that of Gregory the Great, preserved vainglory as a deadly sin, while others incorporated it into pride. The ancient rule of the Anchorites followed the latter course, identifying vainglory (which it defined as "a high opinion of something of one's own and the wish for fame on account of it") as one of various expressions of pride. (Incidentally, while Gregory the Great is considered the author of the seven deadly sins formula, his own schema actually included eight sins—he viewed pride as the source of all sin, including the seven deadly sins.)

The official list of seven deadly sins that has come down to us includes the following (the order has also become standard): Pride, Envy, Anger, Sloth, Greed, Gluttony, and Lust. This is the list that earlier generations of Roman Catholics were taught, and it is the list that popular literature, such as the detective novels of Lawrence Sanders, continues to employ. From time to time, individuals have modified the list, usually by augmenting it. Thus

5. *The Ancrene Riwle*, trans. M. Salu (Notre Dame, Ind.: Univ. of Notre Dame Press, 1956). Also Geoffrey Chaucer, *The Canterbury Tales* (New York: Avenel Books, 1985), 561–63. For a very readable account of the development of the deadly sins schema from Evagrius to Thomas Aquinas, see Mary Louise Bringle, *Despair: Sickness or Sin?* (Nashville: Abingdon Press, 1990), 51–67.

Karl Menninger's chapter in *Whatever Became of Sin*, entitled "The Old Seven Deadly Sins (And Some New Ones)," adds affluence, waste, cheating, stealing, lying, and cruelty.[6] In similar fashion, the novelist Stefan Kanfer contends that the holocaust perpetrated by the Nazi regime teaches us that the eighth sin is the sin of forgetting, and Lance Webb added the sin of anxiety, which pioneers in the modern pastoral theology field associated with guilt.[7]

There have also been attacks on the official list of deadly sins, especially by Roman Catholics, or former Roman Catholics, who were schooled in the traditional list and later came to distrust the ecclesiastical system with which the list was identified. A good example of this reaction is Mary Daly, who contends that the traditional deadly sins system is not what it purports to be— it actually functions as an unspoken but very powerful code of virtue among males.[8]

Protestants have taken less interest in the deadly sins formula because they have identified it with Roman Catholicism, and, more specifically, with the Catholic confessional and catechetical system, which Protestants have traditionally rejected and even denounced. Also, Protestants have tended to focus on the sinful condition as such, attempting to find ways to describe this condition (as rebellion against or estrangement from God, as personal and spiritual bondage, as profound isolation from ourselves and others, as the distortion of our perceptions of reality); therefore they have been much less interested in identifying the specific sins that are reflective and symptomatic of the sinful condition. Indeed, Paul Tillich argued that a focus on individual sins is a

6. Karl Menninger, *Whatever Became of Sin?* (New York: Hawthorn Books, 1973), 133–72.
7. Stefan Kanfer, *The Eighth Sin* (New York: Berkeley Pub. Corp., 1978); Lance Webb, *Conquering the Seven Deadly Sins* (Nashville: Abingdon Press, 1955).
8. Mary Daly, *Gyn/Ecology: The Metaethics of Radical Feminism* (Boston: Beacon Press, 1978), 30–31; idem, *Pure Lust: Elemental Feminist Philosophy* (Boston: Beacon Press, 1984), x.

perversion of the Christian faith, as it tends to trivialize our deep estrangement from God, from ourselves, and from other selves.[9]

William James, however, suggested that this debate over Sin versus sins might be a cultural matter. For example, "the Latin races" have looked on evil "as made up of ills and sins in the plural, removable in detail," while "the Germanic races have tended rather to think of Sin in the singular, and with a capital S, as of something ineradicably ingrained in our natural subjectivity, and never to be removed by any superficial piecemeal operations." James acknowledged that such comparisons of national and ethnic groups are always open to exception, "but undoubtedly the northern tone in religion has inclined to the more intimately pessimistic persuasion."[10]

The Bible offers considerable warrant for a deadly sins system, both in form and content. The lists of serious sins (2 Cor. 12:20; Gal. 5:19-20) indicate that the classification of sins was occurring in the very first century of the Christian era. Also, as various authors have pointed out, the Bible has numerous references to each of the deadly sins, the book of Proverbs being perhaps the richest source in this regard.[11] Given these biblical warrants for

9. Thus, in commending depth psychology and existentialism for bringing to theology something that it always should have known but that it had forgotten and covered up, Tillich noted that depth psychology and existentialism were responsible for the "rediscovery of the meaning of the word 'sin' which had become entirely unintelligible by the identification of sin with sins, and by the identification of sins with certain acts that are not conventional or not approvable. Sin is something quite different. It is universal, tragic estrangement, based on freedom and destiny in all human beings, and should never be used in the plural. Sin is separation, estrangement from one's essential being. That is what it means; and if this is the result of depth psychological work, then this of course is a great gift that depth psychology and existentialism have offered to theology" (*Theology of Culture*, ed. Robert C. Kimball [New York: Oxford Univ. Press, 1964], 123).

10. William James, *The Varieties of Religious Experience* (New York: New American Library, 1958), 117.

11. See Donald Capps, *Life Cycle Theory and Pastoral Care* (Philadelphia: Fortress Press, 1983), 106.

the deadly sins schema, we have no solid rationale for ignoring or neglecting this or similar schemas. In fact, now that the schema is no longer so closely identified with what had come to be a repressive ecclesiastical structure and tradition, we should be able to recognize that it belongs to all Christians, as it predates not only the Reformation but also the schism of Eastern and Western Christianity into its Orthodox and Catholic branches.

While I agree with Tillich that the deadly sins formula is always in danger of trivializing our situation of profound estrangement, I also believe that individuals and groups can use it to identify the attitudes, habits, and traits that especially reflect our estranged condition. Contemporary theologians—most notably, Dorothee Soelle—identify certain traditional deadly sins (e.g., apathy) as clear evidence of that condition.[12]

It is useful to restore Evagrius and Cassian's original view that there are eight, not seven, deadly sins. Apathy and melancholy ought to be distinguished, for each is clearly a deadly sin in its own right. The advantages derived from assigning a deadly sin to each day of the week are not a sufficiently compelling reason to eliminate one of the sins from the official list. Therefore, the schema with which I work includes eight deadly sins: pride, envy, anger, greed, gluttony, lust, apathy, and melancholy.

When linked to one of the most influential developmental theories of our time, Erik Erikson's life-cycle theory, this schema supports the view that deadly sins are personally destructive because they become long-standing habits and even enduring personality traits.[13] Erikson suggests that the normal human life span consists of eight ages or stages: infancy, early childhood, the play age, the school age, adolescence, young adulthood, adulthood, and mature adulthood. Each of these life stages has a dynamic conflict, involving what Joan Erikson has termed a "systonic" and a "dystonic" tendency.[14] For infancy, it is the conflict

12. Dorothee Soelle, "Sin and Estrangement," in *Choosing Life* (Philadelphia: Fortress Press, 1981), chap. 2.
13. E. H. Erikson, *CS*, chap. 7.
14. J. M. Erikson, *Wisdom and the Senses*, 77–78.

of basic trust vs. basic mistrust; for early childhood, autonomy vs. shame and doubt; for the play age, initiative vs. guilt; for the school age, industry vs. inferiority; for adolescence, identity vs. identity confusion; for adulthood, generativity vs. stagnation; and for mature adulthood, integrity vs. despair and disgust.

The distinct value of linking the deadly sins to these life stages and their dynamic conflicts is that one can view sins as enduring habits and traits, developed over time, and not merely, as in a days-of-the-week model, as discrete acts which, one assumes, may be terminated if one simply has sufficient willpower. Thus, in recognizing the deadly sins as enduring habits and traits, the developmental model combats the danger of using the deadly sins system to trivialize our situation of profound estrangement. Its effect is precisely the reverse: it claims that a deadly sin may become central to, or characteristic of, an individual's whole approach to life, both self-defining and self-defeating. Thus, in a developmental perspective, the deadly sins are clearly associated with the self, with that which endures through the stages of life and constitutes our essential identity, what Erik Erikson calls one's "sense of 'I,' "[15] and what Kohut and Wolf describe as "an independent center of initiative" (DSTT, 178).

Deadly sins and life-cycle stages may be correlated as follows: gluttony for infancy; anger for early childhood; greed for the play age; envy for the school age; pride for adolescence; lust for young adulthood; apathy for adulthood; and melancholy for mature adulthood.[16] Assigning a deadly sin to a particular stage of the life cycle does not mean that the sins occur only in these periods of life, but that they have special prominence during this period, figuring decisively in the psychodynamics of this particular stage. This correlation also implies that adults have a larger repertoire of sinful habits and traits than children do, and are able to combine them in ways that intensify their destructive effects. Conversely,

15. Erik H. Erikson, *Identity: Youth and Crisis* (New York: W. W. Norton, 1968), 216–21; idem, "The Galilean Sayings and the Sense of 'I'," *Yale Review* 70 (1981): 321–62.
16. See Capps, *Deadly Sins*, chaps. 2–5.

if younger children already manifest, as habits or traits, the sins assigned to later adult stages, one may assume that the child is experiencing greater emotional distress than is appropriate or acceptable at this age.

Erik Erikson's view that the life stages reflect an epigenetic ground plan, with every stage existing in principle from the very beginning of life, supports the traditional Christian conception of sin as preexistent (or "original"). At the same time, it allows for a more contemporary view, supported by developmental theory, that specific dispositions to sin are psychodynamically based, and that sinful habits and traits arise out of conflictual situations that are inevitably part of the human life cycle.

The Empirical Study

In the empirical study of laity and clergy attitudes toward the eight deadly sins, a three-page questionnaire was sent to both groups. Half of the questionnaire concerned the deadly sins, while the other half concerned the "schedule of virtues" proposed by Erik Erikson, with a virtue assigned to each of the life stages.[17] The questionnaire was presented as a "Life Attitudes Survey," and the fact that the deadly sins schema was being investigated was not directly revealed. This was not because I wanted to trick or deceive the respondents, but because I wanted them to respond to the descriptions provided rather than to names or labels. For example, some might have ranked pride first not because the description led them to do so, but because they were aware that pride has traditionally been viewed as chief among the deadly sins.

The questionnaire was rather simple in design. First, the eight deadly sins (represented as attitudes) were briefly described, and

17. Erik H. Erikson, "Human Strength and the Cycle of Generations," in *Insight and Responsibility* (New York: W. W. Norton, 1964), 111–57.

the respondents were asked to indicate which attitude they considered the worst (i.e., most destructive or damaging). Next, they were asked to circle the one attitude with which they, personally, most closely identified ("The attitude about which you would say, 'This, unfortunately, describes me all too well,' or 'This is the attitude that I have especially struggled to overcome' "). Subjects were then asked to consider the same list of descriptions and indicate whether, in each case, they considered an attitude more characteristic of men or of women, or equally characteristic of men and women. The same procedure was followed for the virtues.

The descriptions of each deadly sin were formulated as follows. First, preliminary descriptions of each sin were developed from the scholarly and popular literature on the deadly sins. They were then tested with seminary students in three classes, and with a group of laity in a congregation in Philadelphia, who proposed various rewordings. The goal was to write the descriptions in such a way as to insure that they were, indeed, tapping "sins" and not merely unattractive, undesirable, or inappropriate attitudes. Here are the eight descriptions that resulted from these consultations:

Greed: A consuming desire for wealth or affluence, causing one to think of little else.

Lust: An abusive and manipulative attitude toward persons of the other sex, treating them as objects or pawns.

Pride: A self-centered attitude where one is continually expecting or demanding praise and adulation.

Anger: An angry or resentful attitude reflected in feelings of strong or intense hostility, vengefulness, and inner rage.

Gluttony: Addictive habits, like excessive or erratic eating and drinking, which cause oneself and others untold misery.

Envy: A persisting envy of another person or persons who enjoy special advantages or receive the attention and recognition that one wants for oneself.

Apathy: An apathetic or callous attitude toward life, reflected in an indifference toward the needs and aspirations of others.

Melancholy: A personal bitterness toward life; hatred and disgust for the world and the people with whom one associates.

In the laity survey, bundles of questionnaires were sent to thirty pastors, sixteen to each, for a total of 480 questionnaires. The pastors were requested to have all sixteen questionnaires filled out if possible, and only by members of their congregations. A total of 259 questionnaires were returned, all of which were usable. Subjects ranged in age from 14 to 85, with a mean age of 49 for women and 48 for men. Ninety-seven percent of the women and 94% of the men attend church two or more times per month. Ninety-three percent of the total sample are white; blacks account for 6%. Five denominations were represented (Methodist, Lutheran, Presbyterian, Episcopalian, and Catholic).

The clergy study, based on the same survey sent to the laity, was mailed to about 450 clergy whose names were supplied by students in one of my courses. The response rate was not very good; only 106 questionnaires had been returned by the time I began to work with the data. (A few more came in later.) The 106 completed surveys provide a rather large body of data, however, and the findings provide interesting comparisons and contrasts between laity and clergy.

Ninety of the respondents were men, sixteen were women. A few more denominations were represented than in the laity study, reflecting the diversity of denominations represented in the seminary course. But the preponderance of mainline denominations made a rather close fit between the clergy study and the earlier study of laity.

Laity Responses

Table 1 indicates the laity's judgment as to which sin is the worst. For the worst sin, an equal percentage of women and men—36%— chose melancholy; 24% of the men and 20% of the women chose lust; and 14% of the women, and 14% of the men, chose anger. Among the remaining sins, scores ranged from 10% of the women viewing greed as the deadliest sin to none of the men viewing envy as the deadliest sin. Both men and women ranked pride and envy the lowest (0% to 4%).

In response to the question "With which sin do you most personally identify?," the results were strikingly different. Table 2 indicates that laymen were most troubled by pride (24%); envy and apathy tied for second place (18% each). Women struggled most with envy (33%); next came gluttony (24%); and then pride (18%). Thus, the sins with which men and women personally identify are also the sins they consider the *least* deadly (pride for men, envy for women). Of the three worst sins—melancholy, lust, and anger—significant numbers of respondents personally identify only with anger (11% of the men, 8% of the women). Only 5% of the men and 4% of the women were personally struggling with melancholy; not a single person in the sample admitted to struggling personally with lust. Since our description of lust was carefully worded to reflect the fact that lust is a power issue, having primarily to do with abusive attitudes and behavior toward persons of the other gender, we may assume that a significant degree of denial is occurring here.

This profile indicates that men struggle with certain narcissistic tendencies and needs: the desire for adulation and admiration (pride), the envy of persons who receive the adulation that one covets for oneself, and an attitude of apathy or lack of zest for life, reflected in indifference toward the needs and aspirations of others. In terms of Bursten's four types of narcissistic personalities, these narcissistic tendencies seem to reflect the more subtle types, i.e., the craving and the paranoid, who experience themselves as emotionally deprived (craving admiration and adulation) and express some resentment over the fact that others,

Table 1

Laity and Clergy Views on Which Sin Is Deadliest

Sins	Laymen (%)	Laywomen (%)	Clergy (%)
Melancholy	36	36	26
Lust	24	20	15
Anger	14	14	11
Gluttony	9	7	4
Greed	8	10	12
Apathy	5	7	16
Pride	3	4	14
Envy	0	3	1

n = 353 (98 laymen; 149 laywomen; 106 clergy)
Columns may total 99 or 101% due to rounding off.

Table 2

Sin with Which Laity and Clergy Most Identify

Sins	Laymen (%)	Laywomen (%)	Clergy (%)
Pride	24	18	42
Envy	18	33	21
Apathy	18	7	3
Gluttony	12	24	11
Anger	11	8	19
Greed	11	6	2
Melancholy	5	4	2
Lust	0	0	0

n = 327 (92 laymen; 136 laywomen; 99 clergy)
Columns may total 99 or 101% due to rounding off.

viewed as less deserving, appear to receive more emotional supplies (thus, critical and suspicious). The more overt types of narcissism are not as much in evidence here. It is possible that the men who were struggling with pride included the exhibitionistic type, as either could be described as possessing "a self-centered attitude where one is continually expecting or demanding praise and adulation." But the craving type, also described by Bursten as highly demanding, fits the description particularly well. That 11% of the laymen personally struggle with greed indicates that manipulation, or the desire to manipulate for personal gain, might be present here as well. Still, the cluster of deadliest sins—pride, envy, and apathy—suggests, for the most part, a profile of the craving and paranoid types.

The women present a similar profile. Two of the sins with which women struggle the most (envy, 33%; pride, 18%) suggest the more subtle forms of narcissism evident in the men, i.e., the craving and the paranoid types. In place of apathy, however, women struggle with gluttony (24%).

Like pride and envy, gluttony is profoundly related to narcissism. Women's struggle with gluttony reveals a deep concern with their bodies, and the sense that one's self-image is mediated in and through the body. A number of women circled the word "eating" in the gluttony description so as to differentiate their struggles with excessive or erratic eating from excessive or erratic drinking. This may simply be an exercise in psychological denial, a refusal to admit to having a drinking problem, but I take it more at face value, as reflecting a concern with the implications of excessive or erratic eating for one's image of self. Also, gluttony is symbolically related to the theme of the hungry self, a major feature of the narcissistic personality.[18] Thus, the women, like the men, struggle with sins that are particularly relevant to narcissism, especially the craving and paranoid types.

The sins with which both men and women are personally struggling are not the sins that they, on objective grounds, consider

18. See Mary Louise Bringle, "Confessions of a Glutton." *The Christian Century* 106, no. 31 (1989): 955–58.

the worst or most deadly. Only 7% of the women considered gluttony the worst sin, only 4% considered pride the worst, and only 3% considered envy the worst. Likewise, only 5% of the men considered apathy the worst, only 3% viewed pride as the worst, and none considered envy the worst. Thus, on objective grounds, the laity do not consider what one might call the sins of narcissism serious, much less deadly; yet, personally and subjectively, they are the sins that trouble the laity the most. While some might view the tendency of respondents to identify personally with sins they judge less dangerous as self-congratulatory or even hypocritical, my own view is that there are better, less cynical explanations. These alternative explanations are presented below.

Certain objections can be raised against the view that the sins with which the laity are personally struggling are the sins of narcissism, or that they reflect struggles that are most characteristic of narcissistic personalities. One obvious objection is that we are engaging here in ex post facto reasoning, and drawing the conclusions that serve our theoretical purposes. One might argue that any of the deadly sins could be construed as a sin associated with narcissism. If respondents had been struggling with greed, for example, it would have been just as possible to relate this proclivity to narcissism, as evidence of the self-aggrandizing tendencies of the narcissistic personality. A similar argument could have been made for anger, for, as we have seen, the narcissistic personality tends to have deep feelings of inner rage. Thus, one might argue, virtually any results for the survey could be used to support an interpretation based on narcissism theory.

There is some truth in this objection, but the issue is not simply whether an individual sin might be connected with narcissism. These profiles for men and women based on three deadly sins indicate not just that narcissism issues are present, but that a particular form of narcissism is involved. The central roles of pride and envy in both women and men's profiles is dramatic evidence that the laity in the study are mirror-hungry personalities who "thirst for self-objects whose confirming and admiring responses will nourish their famished self." Furthermore, their willingness to accept the designation of these sins as something that "unfortunately describes me all too well" or that "I have especially struggled to overcome" indicates, admittedly indirectly, that they believe their hunger for admiration and adulation, and envy of others who receive such admiration and adulation, is something they should learn to cope with and possibly to overcome. That is, they do not feel good about their emotional neediness, and are not a little ashamed that they have these needs and seem unable to satisfy these hungers in a permanent or lasting way. They are no doubt aware of their tendency to take out their emotional neediness on others, to project their self-disgust on others through criticism and faultfinding. According to Bursten, paranoid types want to be treated as special, unlike others. One may assume that the same applies to Christian laity, since so many in the survey ranked envy so high. Thus, the fact that virtually any of the deadly sins could be linked to narcissism is not really the issue. What is important here is that the laity are struggling with certain sins, which reflect particular types of narcissistic personalities.

Another question that might be raised concerns the fact that they answered the question regarding personal struggles with sins *after* they had ranked the eight sins. Could it be that they deliberately chose sins that they had ranked less deadly? If so, this would cast doubt on the validity of their responses. While this is certainly a possibility, it is more likely that laity did not consider pride and envy to be as serious as other sins on the list because these sins do not directly or overtly injure or harm another person. One can swallow one's pride and disguise one's envy, as many of us, from personal experience, well know. In contrast, the sins the laity ranked higher, like melancholy and lust, have direct, destructive effects on other persons. Therefore, pride and envy were not selected as sins one is "personally struggling with" merely because they were ranked as the least deadly. Rather, respondents were saying that they are not currently involved in the destructive acts toward other persons described in the items they ranked the most deadly, but that they *are* struggling with emotions that they feel inside themselves, that they rarely if ever reveal to others, and that they consider somehow to be wrong, even though they may not cause other individuals to suffer: "I should not have this desire for more praise and adulation, and I should not be envious of those who do receive praise and adulation. Why can't I get over these feelings? What is wrong with me that I cannot be content with the attention I *do* receive, and why do I begrudge the attention that others receive, especially since it rarely has a negative impact on my own life?"

In interpreting the laity's responses to the survey, one should recall Kohelet's question, "Who knows the interpretation of a thing?" (Eccl. 8:1). Indeed, who knows. Yet, it seems useful to try to discover how people feel about the deadly sins. While one would have assumed that church-related individuals would be similar to the larger public in some ways, and thus in some manner reflect the narcissistic age in which we live, it is noteworthy that so many of these Christian laity struggle with pride and envy— sins of narcissism, especially of the craving and paranoid types. It is also noteworthy that they do not identify with the more exhibitionistic and manipulative narcissistic types (reflected in their tendency *not* to identify personally with lust and greed). However, the exhibitionistic and manipulative types are who we tend to call "narcissists," so there is the danger that laity struggles with narcissism may go undetected. That they are suffering from its more subtle forms—that is, its more shameful and less gran- diose manifestations—does not alter the fact that they are also narcissistic selves.

Clergy Responses

Table 1 indicates that clergy agreed with the laity that melancholy is the worst sin (26% ranked it first), and that envy is the least deadly sin (only 1% ranked it first). Whereas lust was a clear second to melancholy in the laity survey, it was in a virtual tie for second place with apathy and pride among the clergy (apathy, 16%; lust, 15%; pride, 14%). Surprisingly, clergy did not consider lust to be as deadly as the laity viewed it; 24% of the laymen

(20% of laywomen) and only 15% of the clergy considered lust the deadliest sin.

In their response to the question concerning their own personal struggles with sin, Table 2 indicates that 42% of the clergy ranked pride first. This struggle with "a self-centered attitude where one is continually expecting or demanding praise and adulation" may reflect some exhibitionistic narcissism (after all, the ministry is a profession that enables some to indulge in exhibitionism and reckless acts of bravery that often spell professional suicide). But my sense is that the narcissism they are experiencing is of the craving, emotionally hungry type. While the ministry holds out the promise of a certain amount of praise and approbation for a job well done, ministry is also a profession in which selflessness and thankless service are expected, and where one is often the object of criticism, faultfinding, and negative assessment. Thus, the minister is especially vulnerable to self-depletion. Pride, then, is something that the minister genuinely struggles against, and, as clergy rankings of this deadly sin suggest, ministers consider it a greater danger to one's self than laity do (14% vs. the laity's 3-4%).

The second-ranked sin that clergy personally struggle with is envy (21%). Thus the tendency among laity to struggle with the major sins of certain types of narcissism is found with clergy as well, i.e., the craving and paranoid types. Unlike the male laity, however, few clergy struggle with apathy (only 3% as compared with 18%), and, in contrast with female laity, only 11% of the clergy struggle with gluttony—sins that are part of the constellation of laymen and laywomen's narcissism. Instead, 19% of the clergy struggle with anger. Since anger, especially in the form of resentment, is very much an aspect of the narcissistic personality, the clergy appear to be struggling with narcissistic needs here as well. While the number of women clergy in the sample was too small to warrant comparisons between clergymen and clergywomen, I did check to see whether clergywomen in the survey could possibly be responsible for the clergy's greater tendency to struggle with anger. When the clergywomen are removed from the clergy survey, the percent of clergy struggling with anger remains the same (19%). This confirms that substantially more clergymen than laymen are struggling with anger.

It appears that, whereas other males respond to self-deprivations with apathy or indifference, the clergy (85% male) respond instead with anger. (Note that depression and anger are commonly linked in the clinical literature on narcissism, since depression is often a cover for deep feelings of anger and rage.) This tendency toward anger rather than apathy may be due to the fact that clergy are in a profession in which apathy is considered unacceptable; ministers are expected to be supportive and helpful, and to maintain a hopeful attitude in the face of adversity. Having been assured in Clinical Pastoral Education (CPE) that it is "OK to be angry," clergy find anger to be a more acceptable, if no less painful or potentially destructive, response to self-depletions than apathy. Also, while apathy is more likely to be treated by others as "passive-aggressive" (an attitude of, "If I cannot have what I want, then I'll be damned if I will help others get what they want"), anger enables one to disguise resentment of others more successfully, especially through the avenue of inner rage. Open hostility and vengefulness, because they are widely perceived as inappropriate for all Christians, especially clergy, are less likely channels for clergy resentment. Anger, as clergy are taught in CPE, may be "expressed" (i.e., one's inner rage may be released through appropriately chosen words in constructive ways), but this is precisely so that clergy will not engage in hostilities, the settling of scores, acts of revenge, and the like.

Thus, since the majority of the clergy in this sample were men, and would therefore have been expected to share the laymen's personal struggle with apathy, the results of the survey suggest that clergy, by virtue of their profession, are not allowed to become apathetic or indifferent toward the needs of others, or at least to admit to such indifference, and are therefore likely to take their resentments out in anger instead. Given the fact that clergy experience anger along with pride and envy, it is not unreasonable to assume that they become angry when their needs for admiration and adulation, which in the vast majority of instances are legitimate and not inordinate, go unmet, or when others receive the adulation that they seek for themselves. As only 2% of the clergy admit to personal struggles with greed (as opposed to 11% of the laymen), clergy probably do not greatly resent others who enjoy a higher standard of living than they do, though certainly many resent other *clergy* who enjoy a higher standard of living but do not work any harder than those whose standard of living is lower.

More importantly, clergy do seek the mirroring that narcissistic personalities crave, but many apparently do not receive it. They want to be admired and praised for what they do, but they do not want to demand it, or beg for it. They want it to come unsolicited, to be offered in a genuine and heartfelt manner. They are *not* desirous of being numbered among those narcissists that Kohut and Wolf describe as always "fishing for compliments" (DSTT, 194). On the other hand, it is impossible to determine from the data the extent to which the clergy's anger is due to lack of adulation, or to resentment that they are not allowed to enjoy and take pleasure in one of the few rewards of their profession, namely, the experience of basking in praise and compliments without feeling terribly wrong about it.

The clergy's anger seems to be part of a narcissistic constellation that also includes pride and envy. Kernberg's description of the narcissist's depressive reaction undoubtedly applies to many clergy: "When abandoned or disappointed by other people they may show what on the surface looks like depression, but which on further examination emerges as anger and resentment, loaded with revengeful wishes, rather than real sadness for the loss of a person whom they appreciated" (*BCPN*, 229). Since clergy are often in the situation of being abandoned, of being the victims of broken promises, it is not surprising that they are often angry and resentful, and secretly entertain revengeful wishes toward those who have abandoned or betrayed them.

While the number of women clergy in the sample was too small to justify comparisons with the clergymen, there is some evidence in the data to suggest that clergywomen view apathy rather than melancholy as the deadliest sin, and do not rank pride nearly as high as the clergymen do. Concerning their personal struggles, the profiles are similar (i.e., they too struggle with pride and envy), but more clergywomen appear to struggle with gluttony, so their profile is quite similar to that of laywomen.

The Narcissist as Tragic Self

The purpose in presenting these data has been to show that narcissism is not only "out there" in the culture but also "in here," among practicing Christians. Of course, individuals in the survey who identified themselves as struggling with pride, envy, apathy, gluttony, or anger are not narcissistic in the clinical sense; just because they identify with one of these deadly sins does not necessarily mean that they would manifest the whole range of characteristics reflective of the narcissistic personality. But the data do suggest a distinct tendency of the sample as a whole to struggle with narcissistic needs.

The data also reveal some ambiguity in the minds of respondents as to whether these narcissistic needs are wrong, and, if so, what is to be done about it. On the one hand, since respondents were asked to identify the "life attitude" that "describes me all too well" or that "I have especially struggled to overcome," they do consider that attitude to be wrong for them, and would like to be rid of it if possible, or at least reduce its influence in their lives. On the other hand, because they did not rank these attitudes very high, and therefore did not consider them to be among the more serious sins, they apparently do not consider them to be morally reprehensible, matters that they should feel deeply guilty about. On the contrary, pride and envy are often considered defensible, because, in many instances, they are the sins of persons who have been treated unfairly or shabbily in life, who are the victims of poor parenting, of unfair social practices and policies, or of racial, gender, class, ethnic, and professional prejudices. Actual or perceived differential treatment of siblings by parents may also be involved. Why do others receive all the adulation?

Why am I never praised for my efforts? Why do these others have all the advantages and I have to work for everything I achieve?

It is impossible to judge, on the basis of this study, whether the respondents construe the sins of pride and envy in this way. Yet, since respondents seemed to take the manifest destructiveness of sins into account in their rankings, this is a plausible explanation for why pride and envy are ranked low but are so high on respondents' lists of sins with which they personally struggle. What the present findings do show, quite conclusively, is that because the respondents tend to identify personally with the sins they consider the *least* serious, they are unlikely to experience a great deal of guilt over these personal weaknesses (this is especially true of pride and envy); these are weaknesses that do not have any obvious victims besides themselves, and do not, or need not, do anyone else any direct harm. The one who is most likely harmed by attitudes of pride and envy (also by apathy, gluttony, and even anger) is oneself. Contrast these sins with greed or lust, which have a direct causal link to harm to others.

Nonetheless, it is highly significant that respondents are "struggling against" these sins, trying to overcome them. Why do they wish to overcome them when, for the most part, they consider them to be the less deadly sins? Perhaps because they sense that one ought to be able to live above one's petty feelings of pride and envy, one's needs for admiration and adulation. One should be glad for others when they are recognized for their abilities and achievements, and one should not be disappointed when one's own achievements are overlooked, for, after all, the achievement is its own reward. In the language of narcissism theory, one part of us is telling the other part that it is inappropriate to be "mirror-hungry." One should be satisfied with the small scraps of recognition that come one's way. But the other part of us protests: "But such recognition and admiration is what I live for. Is it self-centered of me to want my share of praise, my moments in the spotlight?" The self engages in an internal debate, questioning itself, even perhaps quarreling with itself, but for the most part coming to no real resolution. The self, after all, can see the validity of both points of view.

The problem is exacerbated for the clergy, for, as Reinard Nauta has recently shown in a study of Dutch clergy,[19] clergy tend to attribute positive outcomes in ministry to themselves and their own efforts, whereas they attribute negative outcomes to external circumstances. Nauta concludes that negative outcomes have a self-protective bias, whereas positive outcomes have a self-enhancing effect. But negative outcomes were attributed to stable, definable factors, such as task difficulty, and positive outcomes were attributed to variable and ambiguous factors (the clergy recognized that they could not take full credit for positive outcomes, for, "With a theological doctrine of divine grace and human fallibility, taking all credit personally for positive outcomes would be considered hubris").[20] Therefore, according to Nauta, clergy were caught in the classic "double bind" of wanting to be recognized for their successes, but having to disclaim any desire for such recognition.

I doubt, therefore, that the respondents to the survey suffer from the narcissism of exhibitionistic grandiosity—the kind of narcissism found among celebrities and other public figures who believe that their rather modest personal achievements rival those of Shakespeare and Lincoln. Rather, it is the narcissism of a self (largely Bursten's craving type) that is struggling with questions and doubts as to how much attention and admiration is enough, and how much is more than one should want or expect. An earlier era probably would have viewed these questions and doubts as evidence of an obsessive personality, caught up in a mind game from which there is no relief. But narcissism theory indicates that the respondents are not obsessive—a neurosis— they have a self-problem. We wonder what is wrong with us that we are so dependent upon the praise and adulation of others, that

19. Reinard Nauta, "Task Performance and Attributional Biases in the Ministry," *Journal for the Scientific Study of Religion* 27, no. 4 (1988): 609–20.
20. Ibid., 619.

we long so for their admiring and confirming response. And we wonder what is wrong with us that we are so profoundly envious when someone else receives the praise and adulation that we have wanted, sometimes so very desperately, for ourselves. These are the questions that those of us who are "mirror-hungry" ask ourselves. These questions are not constantly on our minds, but when they do arise, they are distressing, even painful, for they seem to penetrate to the very core of the self, and the very asking of these questions leaves the self feeling more depleted than before. Awareness of our mirror-hunger rarely makes us feel good about ourselves; on the contrary, it always makes us feel bad or worse.

In short, the respondents to the survey indicate that they wish they were not so hungry for mirroring and that they could take a more disinterested attitude when others receive the adulation they covet for themselves. The whole mirroring experience seems not to have been a very happy one for the vast majority of these respondents. It has been far more disappointing than satisfying, perhaps because they were raised by parents who were unable or unwilling to give them the emotional nourishment they needed. This may be why they can readily accept the idea that the desire for admiration and adulation is an expression of self-centeredness. In any event, some at least say that they would like to reduce their dependence on mirroring, for the failure of one's desire for mirroring, or the observation of someone else receiving the mirroring that one desires for oneself, leaves the self feeling more depleted than ever.

As Kohut and Wolf point out, such mirroring failures typically arouse a deep sense of shame as one realizes that longings for and anticipations of such mirroring will not be met (DSTT, 190). We overestimate the regard that someone else had for us, and we are terribly crestfallen. Remember, in grade school, when Ms. Johnson, handing back papers she had graded, said, "There's someone in the class who did a wonderful job," and remember how you felt when that someone turned out to be someone else? According to Kohut and Wolf, this is the shame that accompanies unmet expectations of mirroring, when the balloon our grandiosity floated suddenly deflates, leaving us more miserable than ever. Such shame is often so painful, so self-depleting, that we are likely to suppress our desire for mirroring, and to resort instead to hopeless withdrawal (DSTT, 190).

We grasp at admonitions from well-intentioned Christians against self-centeredness, for they confirm that it was wrong for us to seek recognition and adulation. What was a display of healthy narcissism is redefined as an expression of self-centeredness, and the Christian faith is used to legitimate the renunciation of our desire to be mirrored. This is tragic, for mirroring is at the very heart of the Christian gospel. Quite simply but profoundly, it is the form and means by which the depleted self experiences divine grace, the benediction of God: "May the Lord's face shine upon you, and give you peace, now and forevermore."

The Threat of Melancholy

What is ultimately at stake in this attempt to eliminate or withdraw one's expectations of being adequately mirrored? Why should one moderate the desire for admiration and adulation? One reason often given, that "pride often goeth before a fall," may well be a factor. The experience of exhibitionistic narcissists who were destroyed by their reckless bravery is often noted in support of this adage. But a more profound reason for such efforts to moderate or regulate one's neediness, to control one's demands, concerns a more realistic threat for craving and paranoid narcissists, namely, the threat of melancholy.

In the survey, melancholy was overwhelmingly judged to be the most deadly sin (36% of the laity and 26% of the clergy), and this was true for all the age groups represented in the laity survey: young, middle, and mature adults (see Table 3). I believe that respondents viewed melancholy as the state into which they hoped they would never fall, for such a state would indeed be a living hell, both for themselves and for the people, especially family members, with whom they associate. It is the sinful state for which few of us have much tolerance when we see it in other persons; it is a form of sinfulness that is almost unpardonable. To be sure, we are prepared to acknowledge that some people, owing to life experiences (debilitating illness, major tragedies, and so forth), have "every right to be bitter." But, even in such cases, we wonder if the bitterness is not somehow excessive, for we can point to other persons who have had similar life experiences and who have not become so bitter.

Table 3

Sin Perceived as Worst by Three Adult Age Groups (Laity)

Sin	20–39 Age Group	40–59 Age Group	60–85 Age Group
Melancholy	33	42	39
Lust	25	20	14
Anger	23	10	10
Apathy	5	7	4
Gluttony	6	10	6
Greed	6	6	19
Pride	1	4	3
Envy	0	1	4
	(n = 79)	(n = 89)	(n = 69)

Respondents to the survey are determined that they will never succumb to such personal bitterness, and are therefore mindful of signs of any susceptibility to this eventuality. From this perspective, pride (with its demandingness), envy and anger (with their resentfulness), gluttony (with its personal miseries), and apathy (with its indifference to others) may leave one vulnerable to the most destructive sin of all, the sin of melancholy. Unlike the other sins, which are habits or traits, melancholy is a condition, and, once it takes hold, it is almost impossible to overcome.

Why did melancholy receive such overwhelming support as the worst sin?

William James suggests that the worst form of spiritual sickness is melancholy, and he cites the example of Leo Tolstoy:

> In Tolstoy's case the sense that life had any meaning whatever was for a time wholly withdrawn. The result was a transformation

in the whole expression of reality. When we come to study the phenomenon of conversion or religious regeneration, we shall see that a not infrequent consequence of the change operated in the subject is a transfiguration of the face of nature in [one's] eyes. A new heaven seems to shine upon a new earth. In melancholics there is usually a similar change, only it is in the reverse direction. The world now looks remote, strange, sinister, uncanny. Its color is gone, its breath is cold, there is no speculation in the eyes it glares with.[21]

Here James describes a world that fails to mirror the self. Melancholy, then, is the result of inadequate or nonexistent mirroring. To become melancholic means to lose one's belief that one is the object of recognition, that one is not only see-er but also seen. As Erik Erikson points out, the narcissism that views the world, or a significant part of the world, as a benevolent face is a "certified narcissism," and is not to be confused with the narcissism of self-promotion and self-inflation that the moralists condemn.[22] Such certified narcissism is ultimately grounded in our experience of God as luminous and aglow, as when we ask that God's face would shine upon us and give us peace. The melancholic, of course, does not know such peace, for melancholia is truly the condition of estrangement: from self, from world, from God.

Thus the survey respondents' concern about the sins of narcissism is not only understandable but tragically legitimate. They are concerned, in effect, that the demandingness of the craving self and the resentment of the paranoid self could, if not checked, clear the way for melancholy, a personal bitterness toward life and a hatred and disgust for the world and the people with whom one associates, at home and work. It is tragic that legitimate desires for admiration and adulation, and legitimate concerns that we are deprived of emotional supplies that we deserve as much as others do, are being relinquished due to fears of becoming

21. James, *Varieties*, 129.
22. Erik H. Erikson, *Toys and Reasons* (New York: W. W. Norton, 1977), 87.

bitter later in life. One can almost hear the sigh of anguish and despair that accompanies these acts of resignation and renunciation. But in an era in which the mirror is painted black, what other choice is there? We live, as Kohut says, in an era not of the guilty self but of the tragic self.[23]

The Need for Mirroring

What implications might one draw from the survey for life among Christians? After years of practicing psychoanalytic detachment and carefully avoiding the dangers of countertransference, Kohut began to realize that what his patients needed most was mirroring.[24] They needed him to respond affirmatively to their self-idealizations, even if these took a rather grandiose form, and they needed him graciously to accept the idealizations that they held of him, not merely to assume that they were being manipulative or seductive. He realized that they desperately needed mirroring, and he began to advocate that analysts give mirroring responses. Unfortunately, he chose a weak, inadequate word to describe the mirroring responses of the analyst, the word "empathy," which had already been widely promoted by Carl Rogers and the client-centered school of psychotherapy.[25]

Empathy—"feeling with" the patient or client—does not adequately capture what is involved in the mirroring of the other's desire to be admired and to admire, nor does it adequately communicate that such desire for mirroring is for the purpose of overcoming deeply rooted feelings of self-depletion. Yet, if the word for this intervention on the part of the analyst is inadequate,

23. See Kohut's discussion of the tragic vs. guilty self in *RS*, 206–7 and 224–25. Also, see his essay, "On Courage," in Heinz Kohut, *Self Psychology and the Humanities*, ed. Charles B. Strozier (New York: W. W. Norton, 1985), esp. 37–45.
24. See Kohut's discussion of mirroring in *AS*, 115–18; idem, *How Does Analysis Cure?* (Chicago: Univ. of Chicago Press, 1984), 143–44.
25. See Carl R. Rogers, "The Characteristics of a Helping Relationship," in *On Becoming a Person* (Boston: Houghton Mifflin, 1961), 39–58.

the intervention itself is critically important to the patient's restoration and healing.

Pastors and parishioners need to give more systematic attention to the mirroring that may appropriately occur between them. To explore the many implications of this proposal for ministry in general, and pastoral care in particular, or to cite the ways in which such mirroring is already taking place in pastoral ministry, would be a book in itself. But we may locate this mirroring theme within the larger, theological context provided by Erik Erikson in *Toys and Reasons*, where he notes the affinities between the greeting ritual of mother and infant in the morning and the relationship we have with God. As the mother greets her infant by name, as she lifts the child up, and as her face reflects her infant's joy of seeing her, so, according to Erikson, does God greet us by name and lift us up, and we sense the joy and warmth of the glow on God's face that corresponds to our own. As Erikson points out, this mirroring event is ritually affirmed in the sacrament of baptism, and repeated in the funeral service, when our spirit is declared to have been lifted up to heaven.[26]

What this means for pastors, and pastoral care, is nicely expressed in the final sermon that John Henry Newman preached before his conversion from the Anglican to the Roman Catholic Church. The sermon was entitled "The Parting of Friends," and, in the closing paragraph, he expressed his hope that he in some degree "has read to you your wants or feelings, and comforted you by the very reading; has made you feel that there was a higher life than this daily one, and a brighter world than that you see."[27] Here Newman describes a form of mirroring that does more than simply reflect the images projected onto it. Accurate reflecting is vital, but it is never enough, for good mirroring also responds to our need to affirm a brighter world than we had known, when the room was dark and the light was dim or absent.

26. Erikson, *Toys and Reasons*, 85–92.
27. John Henry Newman, "The Parting of Friends," in *Sermons Bearing on Subjects of the Day* (London: Longmans, Green, and Company, 1909), 395–409 [quotation is on p. 409].

Is not this brighter world the new heaven and new earth that the author of the book of Revelation envisions when he proclaims: "And night shall be no more; they need no light of lamp or sun, for the Lord God will be their light, and they shall reign for ever and ever" (Rev. 22:5). This is no grandiose fantasy, but the assurance that we are the gleam in God's eye, that we are God's beloved, in whom God is well pleased, and that we therefore have no reason to fear that our life-world will lose its color, for it will always be bathed in the light of God's luster. The reliable mirroring that occurs between pastor and parishioners—meeting the needs of both—is, indeed, must, be rooted in the mirroring activity of God—the God revealed through Jesus, whom the author of Revelation calls "the bright morning star" (22:16). We are tragic selves, but this is all the more reason why we should do what we can for one another to forestall the day when the world turns sinister, its eyes cold and glaring.

4

Sin in a
Shame-Based
Theology

If asked to talk about feelings of pride, envy, anger, and so forth, many people would probably use the language of guilt: "I feel guilty when I demand that others recognize my true worth"; "I feel guilty when I envy his success"; "I feel guilty when I overeat"; "I feel guilty when I get angry and want to get back at people for what they have done to me." Some guilt is undoubtedly involved in each of these cases, but the deeper layer of emotion in these expressions of personal wrongfulness is best described as shame. For the victim in each of these cases is felt to be the self, and the feelings involved express and even contribute to a sense of self-depletion, of self-diminishment. Even as we experience such feelings, we feel low, depressed, vulnerable, empty, or insignificant. We try to rid ourselves of such feelings because we do not like what we are doing to ourselves. Yes, others may be indirectly hurt by our feelings and attitudes, and, for this, we ought to be sorry and repentant. But the primary victim of such feelings and attitudes is the self.

The Experience of Shame

This chapter explains what shame is, so that we can know it when we experience it, and then sketches out a shame theology (in contrast to the traditional guilt theologies), and, more specifically, what sin means or entails in a shame theology. This ambitious undertaking is well worth the effort (even if it means overreaching somewhat), because our age, like all previous ages, calls for a relevant theological response, and today that response needs to focus on the problem of shame.

Shame and Our Image of Self

Chapter 2 alluded briefly to the fact that shame is a response to our failure to live up to an ideal that we have held for ourselves and that shame is therefore the experience of a self-deficiency. Even where this ideal was implanted originally by a parent, it is now self-owned, and thus the shame is a reaction to the failure to live up to one's own self-ideals. We are disappointed in ourselves. We have once again let ourselves down, and we are puzzled and angry at ourselves: "Why do I do this to myself?" This reaction is quite different from guilt, for, with guilt, the ideals that we have failed to live up to we continue to associate with the expectations of others. If my father wanted me to be a pediatrician or to succeed him as the head of the family firm, and I chose instead to become a minister, I am likely to feel some guilt over this—I have let him down, I have not met his expectations, and I have knowingly and intentionally done so. Most of us, regardless of our conviction that it was the right thing to do, experience guilt over failing to meet or fulfill a parent's expectations of us.

In recognizing that shame is what we feel when we have failed to meet our *own* expectations, the recent clinical literature on shame emphasizes, as the earlier literature on shame and guilt did not, that shame and the self are intimately related. The recent literature is challenging the earlier view of psychologists, anthropologists, and historians that shame is largely associated with the violation of social norms, whereas guilt is more deeply personal. This older view, which arose out of efforts to compare and contrast "shame cultures" (typically, Asian societies) and "guilt cultures" (Western societies), placed considerable emphasis on the relationship between shame and honor. It claimed that shame results from undergoing the loss of social status, of being held up as an example of a "bad citizen" because one has violated social custom, acting in ways that are inappropriate to one's age, social position, and the like. Thus, shame was viewed as a phenomenon that would be found in hierarchical societies and in societies with a strong commitment to social protocol, rules of etiquette, and the like—customs that were never very strong in the egalitarian and pluralistic societies of the West.[1]

But recent literature on shame has challenged this view. The American historian John Demos claimed that the child-rearing practices of early Puritan settlements in New England reveal that the core psychological experience of Puritans was shame and that guilt was secondary. Demos contended that the Puritan evidence supports Erikson's view that, in many societies, shame is readily absorbed by guilt. What made Demos's claims so striking and challenging is that Puritanism has always been associated with guilt, and has been used to support the claim that America is, and always has been, a guilt-oriented society.[2] I have analyzed

1. See, e.g., Ruth Benedict, *The Chrysanthemum and the Sword: Patterns of Japanese Culture* (Boston: Houghton Mifflin, 1946); and Gerhart Piers and Milton B. Singer, *Shame and Guilt* (Springfield, Ill.: Charles C. Thomas, 1953).
2. John Demos, *A Little Commonwealth: Family Life in Plymouth Colony* (New York: Oxford Univ. Press, 1970), 138–39. See also idem, "Shame and Guilt in Puritan Culture," a paper presented at the Center for Psychosocial Studies, The Psychoanalytic Institute, Chicago, Ill., 1972. It is not surprising that Demos, attuned to the shame dynamics in Puritan society, would also focus on its narcissistic tendencies as well. See especially his analysis of the case of Elizabeth Knapp and her experience of "narcissistic depletion" in *Entertaining Satan: Witchcraft and the Culture of Early New England* (New York: Oxford Univ. Press, 1982), 120–23.

the transcript of the excommunication proceedings against a Boston woman who was hanged as a witch some ten years prior to the Salem witch hangings, and am convinced that the ritual during these proceedings was based on shame dynamics.[3] This analysis and Demos's analysis of Puritan child-rearing practices, however, establish only that shaming was a primary mechanism of social control. The recent clinical literature insists on a further connection: that shame is deeply self-involving and has a profound effect on one's own self-image, not only on how one is perceived and acted upon by others.

The person who did the most to change our understanding of shame was Helen Merrell Lynd, whose book *On Shame and the Search for Identity*, published in 1958, remains the seminal work in the study of shame.[4] Lynd suggests six characteristics of shame, which may be organized around three major themes: the phenomenological experience of shame, the effects of shame on the self, and the effects of shame on one's worldview. A brief summary of her analysis of shame according to these three themes will explain why theorists today view shame as an experience in which one's whole self is involved and is profoundly at risk.

Shame as Self-Involving

Concerning the phenomenological experience of shame (i.e., what it is like to experience shame), Lynd notes that shame involves the total self, and, unlike guilt, cannot be externalized.[5] We *perform* guilty actions, but we *are* our shame. Whereas guilt can be externalized by distancing ourselves from the action—"I did it, yes, but I was not myself"—shame cannot be externalized in this way. When we experience shame, we do not even try to argue,

3. Donald Capps, "Erikson's Theory of Religious Ritual: The Case of the Excommunication of Ann Hibbens," *Journal for the Scientific Study of Religion* 18 (1979): 337–49.
4. Helen Merrell Lynd, *On Shame and the Search for Identity* (New York: Science Editions, 1958), chap. 2.
5. Ibid., 49–56.

to ourselves or to others, that the total self is not involved. With guilt, it is possible that we will successfully rationalize a way out of the situation so that we will not have to take responsibility for it; whereas, with shame, rationalizations and explanations only make self-involvement all the more apparent and all the more painful.

If anything works for shame as rationalization works for guilt, it would be amnesia, the ability to put the experience out of mind. Amnesia is never a perfect solution, however, for the mind has an uncanny ability to remember shame experiences. Most of us can recall only a few childhood experiences. I submit that many of these are experiences of shame. The fact that they were deeply painful is not sufficient to enable us completely to repress them. Fear, or dread, as in the case of incest, would also have to be present for such an experience to be completely obliterated. The more one tries to forget a shameful experience, the more it comes to mind, and each unbidden and unwanted recollection inflicts a stabbing pain.

The totally self-involving nature of shame is also evident in the fact that, unlike guilt, it tends to involve one's body as well as one's mind. Whereas guilt is usually described as felt in the conscience (i.e., the mind), shame is deeply visceral and gut-wrenching; it is usually felt in the pit of the stomach. Shame involves the bodily self, not just the thinking self but also the feeling self, and this is perhaps why shame experiences often have debilitating physical effects, making one lethargic, apathetic, and susceptible to physical illness.

Lynd also points out that shame involves self-exposure, the sense that one has been stripped bare, rendered naked, exposed to the critical gaze of those who happen to be present.[6] Standing as it were in the spotlight, one desperately seeks to sink into the ground, to fall through the floor, to wake up from what one fervently but futilely hopes is a terrible nightmare. While the perception of the disapproving gaze of others is often a feature, and a painful aspect, of shame, an even more devastating feature

6. Ibid., 27–34.

is the "exposure of oneself to oneself." This self-exposure is "at the heart of shame."[7] As a result of a shame experience, we have great difficulty not only facing others but also facing ourselves. When we undergo an especially painful shame experience, we often say that we were unable to look at ourselves in the mirror; the self-recognition would be too difficult to bear.

Thus, to experience shame is to experience, in an unusually deep and painful way, a sense of self-estrangement, a wave of self-rejection, even of self-revulsion. The exposure of ourselves to ourselves is actually worse, therefore, than our exposure to the critical gaze of another. While the others' critical gazes may produce shame, a sense of humiliation, it also tends to evoke rage, a shame projected outward, as in the American ballad that tells of a public hanging where the criminal cursed the crowd of on-lookers, "God damn your eyes."[8] We are more likely to experience pure shame when the one to whom we are exposed is the self, for then we have no opportunity to turn our shame outward in rage toward those who have humiliated us.

Some of the worst shame experiences, then, have nothing at all to do with public humiliation. One may, for example, preach a sermon that the congregation considers good, and yet, in mulling it over afterward, one may suddenly feel a deep sense of shame because the sermon fell far below one's own standards. The ideal self says, "That was not very good and you know it," and the real self rejoins, "I got away with it, and they didn't know the difference." The worst experiences of shame, and the most common experiences of shame, do not concern humiliating ourselves in public, but disappointing or betraying ourselves. Like the woman whose boss's accusatory manner places her on the defensive, and leads her to respond in ways that are not entirely truthful: "I hate myself when I realize that I have lied to him"—this is shame, and it is deeply self-revealing. When put on the defensive, she knows she is likely to resort to lying, and this is not something that she likes about herself. In fact, she hates herself for it.

7. Ibid., 31–32.
8. See Erikson, *CS*, 253.

Shame is also experienced as inappropriate or incongruous. Shame experiences are strangely out of place; they are anomalies, events that should never happen. Usually, they seem senseless because the pain they are able to cause is out of proportion to their significance (as judged by any external or objective test). A pastor I know cannot forget the time when, as a member of a seminary choir, he began his brief solo on the wrong note. This experience, which happened many years ago, is still painful for him to recall. Of course, the audience that was gathered there that night has long since forgotten about it. (Most have probably forgotten that they were even there that night.) But he cannot forget, and every time the experience comes to mind, he feels its painfulness, even though he knows, objectively speaking, that this experience is rather unimportant. To say to him, as I have done, "But think of all the right notes you have sung since that time," evokes a brief laugh, but it is not a hearty laugh—the pain is still there.

Lynd suggests that the incongruity and inappropriateness of shame experiences bring one face-to-face with the senselessness and meaninglessness of human experience in general.[9] A woman who was dying confessed to her pastor that she had told an untruth about another woman so that this woman would not be elected to replace her as the president of the women's group in her church. Ashamed of what she had done, and still feeling pain after all these years, she mused, "Life is silly, isn't it. It seems to make so little sense, somehow."[10]

Writers of autobiography often dwell on their shame experiences, even though, objectively speaking, these are not the most significant experiences in their lives. They do so because these are the very experiences that challenge the assumption that their lives are meaningful. Shame experiences raise doubts that one even has a right to write an autobiography, because the whole

9. Lynd, *On Shame*, 57–58.
10. See Newman S. Cryer, Jr., and John M. Vayhinger, eds., *Casebook in Pastoral Counseling* (Nashville: Abingdon Press, 1962), 60–62.

point of an autobiography is to show that one's life has been meaningful.[11]

Shame experiences do not fit into a meaningful pattern. If life has continuity and structure, if it is an intricate weaving, as Joan Erikson suggests,[12] then shame experiences seem strangely out of place. They pull and tear, and leave embarrassing splotches, defacing what would otherwise be a beautiful work of art. Shame experiences are evidence that one's life has discontinuities, is always on the verge of chaos, is deeply flawed.

Shame as Self-Constricting

Concerning the effects of shame on the self, Lynd points out that shame is a threat to our basic disposition to trust, because a shame experience violates our expectations of what is happening, or about to happen.[13] Shame experiences come without any premeditation or prior warning. Suddenly, we find ourselves in such a situation, and we realize, too late, that we had trusted ourselves to a situation that was not there. If we had known what we were about to encounter, we would have taken appropriate steps to avoid it; in many situations that produce shame, we realize, after the fact, how easily we could have avoided them.

It is significant that shame and confusion are often associated in the Psalms: "Let them be put to shame and confusion altogether who seek to snatch away my life" (40:14; also 35:25, 70:2). As cause of confusion or disorientation, shame undermines our disposition to trust that the world is as we believe it to be. If, as the Eriksons' life-cycle theory asserts, trust is the disposition on

11. Donald Capps, "Parabolic Events in Augustine's Autobiography," *Theology Today* 40 (1983): 260–72; idem, "Augustine's *Confessions:* The Scourge of Shame and the Silencing of Adeodatus," in Donald Capps and James E. Dittes, eds., *The Hunger of the Heart: Reflections on the Confessions of Augustine* (West Lafayette, Ind.: Society for the Scientific Study of Religion Monograph Series, 1990), 69–92.

12. Joan M. Erikson, *Wisdom and the Senses: The Way of Creativity* (New York: W. W. Norton, 1988), chap. 3.

13. Lynd, *On Shame*, 43–49.

which all other life-affirming dispositions are based, the cry "Do not let me be put to shame" is a very basic plea for self-survival. I must be able to trust if I am to live in this world. As Freud put it, we need to know that we cannot fall out of this world.[14]

A seminarian who had agreed to serve as supply pastor on the Sunday when the nation changed from daylight saving to standard time suddenly realized, while en route to the church, that instead of arriving one half hour early, he would be arriving one half hour late! In the world of daylight saving time, he was safe and secure. But he was in the world of standard time, and shame resulted from the fact that he had trusted to a world that was not there.

The seminarian who arrived at church a half hour late has vowed that he will never make this mistake again, and he may well succeed. He will certainly have more shame experiences, but they probably will not involve the failure to make the transition from daylight saving to standard time. This illustrates the frequently self-constricting nature of shame experiences. They cause one to become less spontaneous, less free-spirited, more cautious, more calculating, and less favorably disposed to the element of surprise. Perhaps this is why surprise parties in our honor often make us anxious and uncomfortable. They are too reminiscent of shame experiences in which we trusted ourselves to a situation that was not there and became profoundly self-conscious as a result.

Unfortunately, the effect of shame experiences is to make us more fearful, less willing to take risks, and more concerned for self-survival than for self-expansion and new experience. Shame experiences usually cause us to narrow our life-world, to limit ourselves to a predictable routine, to do the things that we can do easily. This is because the unexpected nature of shame experiences leave the largely false idea that such experiences are most likely to occur when we are taking risks and making ourselves vulnerable. But, if shame experiences continue to occur when we least expect them, then they are actually most likely to

14. Sigmund Freud, *Civilization and Its Discontents*, trans. James Strachey (New York: W. W. Norton, 1961), 12.

occur when we are following a routine, not when we are trying something new and different.

Shame as Tragic Estrangement

Concerning the effects of shame on one's worldview, Lynd says that it brings one in touch with tragedy, especially the tragic aspects of interpersonal relationships.[15] She takes particular note of relationships between family members, and the shame that children feel for their parents, or that parents feel for their children. We want to bring our fiance home to meet our parents, but we are ashamed of our parents, and then we are ashamed of ourselves for feeling ashamed of them. Maybe our parents are uncouth or poorly educated; or maybe mother or dad is mentally disturbed, alcoholic, or drug dependent. Whatever the reasons, we feel shame for them, and then we are ashamed for feeling this way, for we should be able to ignore our parents' shortcomings. Conversely, parents are deeply ashamed of an adult child, whether because the child cannot hold down a job, is involved in criminal or deviant activities, has married beneath their own social and economic level, or committed atrocities in Vietnam.

Lynd notes that "the impact of shame for others may reach even deeper than shame for ourselves,"[16] and, as we feel shame for someone of whom we should, ideally, feel pride and admiration, we are, in that moment, confronted with the tragedy of human existence. Such tragedy is poignantly portrayed in *Night*, Elie Wiesel's account of his experience in a Nazi concentration camp. Realizing that caring for his father was threatening his own chances for survival, Elie, a teenager, experienced the tragedy of human existence through his shame for his father:

> It was daytime when I awoke. And then I remembered that I had a father. Since the alert, I had followed the crowd without troubling about him. I had known that he was at the end, on the brink of

15. Lynd, *On Shame*, 56–63.
16. Ibid., 56.

death, and yet I had abandoned him. I went to look for him. But at the same moment this thought came into my mind: "Don't let me find him! If only I could get rid of this dead weight, so that I could use all my strength to struggle for my own survival, and only worry about myself." Immediately I felt ashamed of myself, ashamed forever.[17]

This is not the tragedy of Oedipus, of the hero-king who is eventually brought down by his guilty actions, but the tragedy of ordinary persons who are ashamed of those with whom their lives are irrevocably intertwined, and who are ashamed of these very feelings of shame. This is the deep tragedy of shame, a tragedy all the more sad and haunting because it is so ordinary and common. The tragedy is that the very persons we ought to admire are those whom we hold in such disrespect. As Kohut suggests, the shameful self is a tragic self, for, unlike the guilty self who has an aura of the heroic, the shameful self feels mean, ungrateful, and resentful that it has been deprived of the mirroring that occurs when there is shared admiration, child for parent, parent for child. The fact that we cherish the one or two occasions in life when parent—and child—dared to express their pride in one another indicates just how tragic are the estrangements brought about by the shame we have for others.

Shame also confronts us with a profound sense of isolation from others, with our aloneness in the world.[18] Shame experiences are difficult to talk about, to communicate to others, and they are difficult for others to hear and listen to. They are difficult to communicate to another for two reasons. One is that to tell another person about a shame experience produces more shame; a shame experience becomes more, not less, shameful to the extent that it is more widely known. Thus, whereas relating a guilty action to another may be cathartic, for such disclosure does not add to one's sense of guilt, the relating of a shame experience actually

17. Elie Wiesel, *Night*, trans. Stella Rodway (New York: Avon Books, 1960), 118.
18. Lynd, *On Shame*, 64–71.

contributes to one's sense of shame. This is one reason why women who are victims of rape keep the experience to themselves; they may not even talk about it with friends, much less report it to the authorities. The assumption that self-disclosure makes a person feel better does not always apply to experiences of shame. Some people have concluded, and for very good reasons, that they will never divulge a certain shame experience to another soul, believing, quite rightly, that such revelation may only make matters worse, that it will not be cathartic or healing. This means that a part of the self, perhaps a part that is central to who one is, remains isolated, unshareable with any other.

The other reason shame experiences are difficult to communicate is that, in telling the story, one reexperiences the shame and the pain that goes along with it. It is virtually impossible to relate a shame experience as though it were over and done with. Much as we relive a traumatic event—a war experience, an automobile accident, an act of violence—each time that it comes to consciousness, so we relive shame experiences as we recall and describe them, and to relive the experience is to relive the pain that accompanied it. This is why we often modify the story in the retelling, eliminating the details that made the experience a shameful one in the first place. If something we said caused the shame experience, then we modify the words, making them just different enough so that, if this modified version were accurate, we would probably not have experienced any shame at all. If we did something that caused the original experience of shame, then, in the retelling, we modify the act just enough so that it no longer contains the feature of our behavior that produced the feelings of shame.

We make such modifications not only because we want to hide from the other person what we actually said or did, but also because we are still engaging in an internal argument over what we have said or done; the ideal self is telling the real self, "If only you had said this, or done this, the whole thing would have been avoided." Thus, we modify the story, because we want so desperately to believe that the event never happened, or, at least, never happened as we remember it. These modifications may create a useful fiction, an imagined alternative to what really happened, but they also reinforce the sense that shame experiences are ultimately incommunicable, thus increasing our sense of isolation and aloneness in the world.

Persons who have experienced shame often feel that they cannot talk to anyone, even the person to whom they are closest. This deep sense of isolation is reflected in the fact that, after a shame experience has occurred, we debate internally whether to tell anyone about it. Though we might not hesitate to relate other painful experiences, even the loss of a loved one, we always hesitate where shame is involved. Thus shame is perhaps the most self-isolating experience. A shame experience may occur in a very public place, but experientially it is always an utterly private affair. In the moment when two lovers experience shame, they experience each other as strangers, and recriminations often follow. It was their shame, not their guilt, that caused Adam and Eve to hide from God and to blame another.

If shame experiences are difficult to relate, they are also difficult to listen to. They tend to render the listener impotent, feeling as though nothing one can say will help. With guilt, the listener is usually able to provide some reassurance: "You didn't really mean to do it"; "It was a learning experience"; "To those who are truly sorry, God promises forgiveness, and the opportunity to make amends." How do we make amends for a shame experience? The primary victim of shame is the self, and there is nothing that one can do by some intentional act (e.g., of confession or atonement) to alleviate the pain. Furthermore, shame is not a learning experience, for what has one learned that one can use in the future? Because shame experiences are like lightning, rarely striking in the same place twice, one cannot prepare for them.

Bereft of the usual reassurances that have some chance of working with those who are experiencing guilt, the listener usually tries to minimize the experience, to point out the discrepancy between its objective reality and the way it has been subjectively experienced. The listener tells us that it was not such a big deal, that not many people noticed, that we are making more of it than the actual circumstances warrant, and that, after all, such experiences have happened to many others. Or, the listener may try to humor us, to tease us gently for taking it so seriously, as when I said to my pastor friend, "But you've sung a lot of right notes since." Yet, such attempts to reassure almost always fall on deaf ears, for we sense intuitively that the only thing that can help is time, and, even with the passage of time, we know that the pain will never completely go away. Thus, the reassuring words of another tend to increase, not decrease, the isolation that we feel. So, if the original experience of shame impressed upon us our estrangement from the self—the inner division or controversy between the ideal and real self—attempts to communicate shame persuade us of our essential estrangement from others.

A Theology of Shame

Clearly, shame is an experience for which our normal coping skills are ineffective. Deprived by shame of our usual methods of combatting life's capacity to injure, forced by shame to confront the possibility that life is without ultimate meaning, and compelled by shame to recognize our estrangement from ourselves and others, we find ourselves in need of healing, of true self-repair. Realizing that simply trying harder, as Bursten describes the efforts of those engaged in narcissistic repair, is ineffectual, we seek the wisdom that theology has traditionally offered to those who are estranged from self, from world, and from God. We turn to theology not as an academic science but as a source of therapeutic wisdom.[19]

Until recently, however, theologians have given little attention to the shame experience. If they considered it at all, they viewed it as earlier generations of anthropologists and historians did, as the violation of social mores and customs, and therefore as a social or cultural issue, and not as an issue of vital importance to our

19. Donald Capps, *Life Cycle Theory and Pastoral Care* (Philadelphia: Fortress Press, 1983), chap. 5.

understanding of Christian faith and life. Gone are the days, however, when we could associate shame with "Confucian cultures," and then proceed to view guilt as the paradigmatic root of human estrangement—from self, from others, from God. In fact, guilt has tended to function as a convenient cover story, enabling Christian theology to ignore the experience of shame and the threat that it poses for the self and its struggle for survival.

This subterfuge begins with the Garden of Eden story, which places an overlay of guilt on an experience that is most profoundly one of shame. The prohibition not to eat of the tree and the decision of the human couple to do so is the cover story of guilt that has distracted readers, including many great theologians, from the crucial event in the story, namely, the shame that the human couple felt in company with one another and before God. Their shame was the real measure and expression of their estrangement from self, from other, and from God. Given the centrality of shame in the story, the prohibition not to eat of the tree is little more than a plot device designed to get the story under way. Otherwise, we must assume that God is a petty and petulant parent who devises meaningless character tests, tests that God's children will necessarily fail.

Therefore, theology cannot afford to dismiss shame, to treat it as a nontheological issue. We now know that theology's failure to concern itself with shame in the past was, in part, the consequence of its own social location. The Western bias of theology led it to view guilt as a deeper experience, precisely because guilt was thought to be more characteristic of Western than of Asian societies, and of societies judged to be more "advanced" and less "backward" and "primitive." The male orientation of theology also led it to view guilt as a deeper experience than shame because, as Helen Lewis points out, guilt is more prevalent among males, whereas shame is more predominant among women.[20] Thus, for decades, even centuries, we have been requiring Christian women

20. Helen Block Lewis, *Shame and Guilt in Neurosis* (New York: International Universities Press, 1971), 153–54.

to interpret their experiences of shame within the conceptual framework provided by the theology of guilt, and therefore to do violence to their own experience; for, as we are now acutely aware, we deny our experience to the extent that we fail accurately to name it. It is incongruous that those of limited power—the women, the children, the elderly—have been engaging, Sunday after Sunday, in confessions of wrongdoing that are more befitting those who wield enormous power. This is not to say that anyone is able to avoid hurting others, whether by thought, word, or deed; nonetheless, it seems strange that those who are most likely to be the victims of shame are also more likely to be engaged in the confession of guilt.

Yet, all of us—men and woman alike—have been victims of the conceptual violence inflicted upon us by theologies of guilt, for all of us have experienced shame. All of us, at one time or another, have tried somehow to accommodate these experiences to a theology of guilt, and have rarely allowed ourselves to trust our judgment that the experiences and the theological meanings we have attached to them are poorly matched. Time and time again, we have tried to assimilate our experiences of shame to a theology of guilt, and when we have intuitively felt that our experience and our theological name for this experience were a poor match, we concluded that there must be something wrong with us, that some weakness in our own minds made it difficult for us to understand the connection, for surely our theological system was not to blame. So let us now recognize what we have not trusted ourselves enough to recognize before, namely, that our theologies of guilt are inadequate, and that we desperately need a theology of shame to take its place alongside theologies of guilt.

Three Problematics of the Self

The theology of shame that I advocate takes its cues from the analyses of shame provided by Lynd and more recent clinical literature. It does not focus on shame as a mechanism of social control, as a means to preserve a hierarchical social structure. Rather, it focuses on the self, and attends to the intimate link between shame and the self, viewing the shame experience as highly illuminative of what we may call the "problematics of the self." The following problematics of the self are illumined by shame:

The Divided Self

We have seen that, in the shame experience, the self experiences itself as divided or split. This division may be described in various ways, each of which highlights different features of the division. For example, it may be characterized as a division between the ideal and the real self. In the shame experience, the real self— the one who acted or was acted upon—has failed to live up to the expectations of the ideal self. Under more normal circumstances, the ideal and the real self may be more congruent, more in harmony with one another. In the shame experience, however, their incongruity becomes painfully evident, and they are set at odds with one another, with the result that the self becomes hesitant, unsure of itself, and immobilized. In "The Divided Self and the Process of Its Unification," William James noted that "the normal evolution of character chiefly consists in the straightening out and the unifying of the inner self."[21] Shame experiences threaten this unity of the inner self, often causing us to feel that we have regressed to an earlier stage in our self-evolution when we were not as congruent as we have subsequently come to believe ourselves to be.

Another way of looking at the issue of self-dividedness is David Winnicott's distinction between the False Self and the True Self. He contends that the "ideal and real selves" may, in fact, be false, for they are "separated from the roots that compose the matrix of psychic structure, leading to an impoverishment of the capacities for play, creativity, and love; these qualities can be achieved

21. William James, *The Varieties of Religious Experience* (New York: New American Library, 1958), 143.

only through a reestablishment of the predominance of the True Self."[22] If we follow this line of reasoning, more is needed than the reconciliation of two conflicting selves, ideal and real—we need to rediscover a True Self that has been buried under the debris of an essentially false existence.

As Stephen Johnson points out, this rediscovery of the True Self is a painful experience and usually requires the assistance of others. Given the fact that the narcissist is generally better defended than other borderline personalities, it often requires "a massive, cumulative failure coupled with supportive therapeutic intervention" to bring the narcissist to the realization that he or she has constructed a false self that is no longer tenable. With this realization, one may experience "extremely aversive feelings of panic, emptiness, and void associated with feeling there is no substance to the self. This direct experience of nothingness, of enfeeblement and fragmentation, is probably the most over-whelming affective experience and, for those narcissists who have any propensity to act out, the most dangerous." As Johnson goes on to point out, however, "it really requires this deep emotional experience to actualize the crucial shift from the use of others to aggrandize and support the false self to the use of others to fund and nurture the real self. When this shift is made, the person can then devote his energy to that mission, which is at once human and heroic, simple and grand."[23]

Still another way to describe the division of the self is Kohut's concept of the bipolar self. One pole is the exhibitionistic, ambitious, or grandiose self. The other is the idealizing self, which is values- and goals-oriented. In his view, the grandiose self is developmentally prior to the idealizing self (*AS*, 25ff.; *RS*, 171ff.). Kohut points out that the sense of the continuity of the self, the sense of being the same person throughout life, emanates from "the abiding specific relationship in which the constituents of the

22. See Arnold Cooper's discussion of Winnicott in "Narcissism," in *EPN*, 122–23.
23. Stephen M. Johnson, *Humanizing the Narcissistic Style* (New York: W. W. Norton, 1987), 57–58.

self stand to each other" (*RS*, 179–80). Thus, for Kohut, either the grandiose or the idealizing self may experience shame, depending on the circumstances. For example, a patient will arrive at a session flooded with shame and anxiety because of a faux pas he felt he had committed:

> He had told a joke that had turned out to be out of place, he talked too much about himself in company, he had been inappropriately dressed, etc. When examined in detail, the painfulness of many of these situations can be understood by recognizing that a rejection occurred, suddenly and unexpectedly, just at the moment when the patient was most vulnerable to it. That is, at the very moment when he had expected to shine and was anticipating acclaim in his fantasies. (*AS*, 230–31)

In such cases, the grandiose self experiences the shame.

The idealizing self experiences shame when it is rejected or disconfirmed. For instance, a student who is confident of his intellectual ability unexpectedly receives a low grade on a term paper. Or a woman who is confident of her ability to make accurate character assessments discovers that the man she is involved with is very different from what she initially believed him to be. The experience of divorce is typically a rejection or disconfirmation of one's idealized self, and thus a shaming experience, for we believed, at some level, that we were capable of holding a marriage together.

Whether it is the grandiose or the idealized self that experiences the shame, the effect is the same. The relationship in which the constituents of the self stand to each other has been disrupted and, at least temporarily, the self that was not directly shamed becomes more assertive as the self that was shamed becomes more passive and demoralized. If the grandiose self has suffered rejection, as in the case of the faux pas at the party, the idealizing self asserts itself, criticizing the grandiose self's judgment for telling an inappropriate joke, for talking too much, for not giving sufficient thought to dress codes, etc. If the idealizing self has suffered the shame, as in the case of an unexpectedly low grade, then the grandiose or exhibitionistic self asserts itself, plotting ways to get revenge against the professor, to humiliate the professor in class, or to prove the professor wrong in the future: "When I receive the Pulitzer Prize one day, I will remind that old bastard of the grade he gave me in English Comp." Thus, the equilibrium that existed between the two poles of the self, and enabled the self to function as an independent center of initiative and perception, has been disrupted by the shame experience, and they no longer function as a unit.

The theologian who has had the most to say about the divided self is Paul Tillich. In "Estrangement and Reconciliation in Modern Thought," he addresses the theme of self-estrangement, which was commonly struck by the depth psychologists of his day, including Freud, Jung, and Fromm: "The self-estranged self is split into two or more selves which, however, remain within the one self."[24] He goes on to say that, for this self-estrangement, the word "self-hate" is appropriate, and the state of reconciliation, i.e., when the two selves are no longer at odds with one another, may be called "self-love." Following Fromm, Tillich contrasts such self-love to selfishness: "selfishness in distinction to self-love is an expression of our dislike for ourselves. It is infinite greediness which never comes to satisfaction because we are insecure about ourselves, not loving ourselves with the love which is reconciliation" (ERMT, 13).

How can the self-estranged personality be reconciled? Following Jung's observation in *Modern Man in Search of a Soul* that "the patient does not feel himself accepted unless the very worst in him is accepted too," Tillich says that we must "accept ourselves at our worst. We must acknowledge the reality of our own neurosis, our unreconciled stage, and not try to rob ourselves of it" (ERMT, 13). In this essay, then, Tillich exhibits great sensitivity to the division that occurs within the self, and recognizes that

24. Paul Tillich, "Estrangement and Reconciliation in Modern Thought," in *The Meaning of Health: Essays in Existentialism, Psychoanalysis, and Religion*, ed. Perry LeFevre (Chicago: Exploration Press, 1984), 12.

such division often expresses itself in an enmity between two or more selves within the self. He also emphasizes that the self's hope for restoration lies in the reconciliation of the conflicting selves, not in the rejection or denial of either one of them.

But Tillich approaches this problem of self-estrangement from the perspective of a theology of guilt. This is reflected in his adoption of Fromm's view that conscience "plays a great role in [the] hostility of modern man against himself," and in his own contention that the struggle against self-estrangement is part of the "genuinely Christian fight against every kind of law as absolute and an acceptance of the power of grace in life, nature, and man" (ERMT, 13–14). The unreconciled feature of the self, its neurotic aspect, is unreconciled and neurotic precisely because it does not reflect, or participate in, radical Christian freedom. It reflects, instead, the escape from freedom, the fearful recourse to law, conformity, and convention.

We cannot discuss in detail the subtleties of Tillich's analysis of the conditions that make for self-estrangement, but simply note here that his analysis is exclusively informed by his theology of guilt. One striking effect of this theological orientation is the rather moralistic tone of his discussion of self-estrangement, evident, for example, in his emphasis on the selfishness that results from self-estrangement, or in his view that one's neurotic side is the worst side. While he emphasizes self-acceptance, he stresses the acceptance of the worst parts of the self (i.e., neuroses), as though there are better parts that are less in danger of nonacceptance.

Within the context of a theology of shame, self-estrangement is strikingly nonmoralistic. Talk about the best and worst parts of the self is avoided; the grandiose and the idealizing selves are not evaluated as best or worst, but are merely different. Also, and more importantly, a theology of shame finds Tillich's solution—acceptance—inadequate, for it basically commends the suspension of negative judgment, whereas a theology of shame, following Kohut, emphasizes the reconciling effects of positive mirroring between the two inner selves that have been at enmity with one another. Self-mirroring is a more powerful and dynamic expression of self-love than is acceptance because it involves a positive regard for the other self, one that eschews any note or form of superiority or condescension. Whereas "acceptance" implies a tolerant attitude toward the weaker self, mirroring says that I cannot live without my other self, that I am lost without the other. Thus, whereas a hierarchy of inner selves seems to be the inevitable corollary of a theology of guilt, a theology of shame views the inner selves as equals. Where such a hierarchy is posited, the reconciliation, the overcoming of self-estrangement, will necessarily entail a magnanimous gesture by a stronger or better self, and acceptance of the weaker self. Where such a hierarchy does not exist, the reconciliation will involve the mirroring of one another, an event or encounter of self-recognition, as each self becomes the gleam in the eye of the other.

Nevertheless, Tillich's formulation of the problem, i.e., that of self-estrangement, is fundamentally sound. In various essays, Tillich talks about the "centered self," which he describes as "the point in which all motives, drives, impressions, insights, and emotions, converge without any one of them determining the center."[25] This center, the very locus of our freedom, is threatened to the extent that we are not fully integrated, and therefore, self-estrangement is a reflection and expression of our sinful condition.

It is not difficult to draw parallels between Tillich's views on the self and those of Kohut. Kohut speaks of the "cohesive self," describes it as "a center of initiative and a recipient of impressions," one that is "cohesive in space and enduring in time" (RS, 99), and contends that what most threatens the self as such a center of initiative is its dis-integration. The difference between Tillich and Kohut, and it is a major one, is in their assessment of what is primarily responsible for the division or breakdown of the self: Tillich emphasizes guilt and Kohut stresses shame. For Tillich, the conflict is between our healthy and neurotic selves, but for Kohut, it is between our grandiose and idealizing selves. These differences are not surprising, for Tillich's theology reflected the age in which it was written, being thoroughly informed

25. Paul Tillich, "What Is Basic in Human Nature?," in *MH*, 187–88.

by a psychoanalytic tradition whose central paradigm for the human condition was the Oedipal conflict, whereas Kohut's work concerns self disorders.

Yet, Tillich may be viewed as a bridge figure between a theology of guilt, on the one hand, and a theology of shame, on the other, precisely because he gives so much attention to the problem of self-estrangement. Noting that the artist "stands, as it were, in proxy for his generation: not only for the general population but even for the scientific investigators of the sociopsychological scene" (*RS*, 286), Kohut points out that the artists of our time—Kafka, O'Neill, Picasso, Pound, Stravinsky—are not concerned with Oedipal themes but with self disorders. Dostoyevski occupies a "specific transitional position," however; his works deal with "structural conflict—with the Oedipus complex and with guilt," and yet "they also depict the fact that it is a weak, crumbling, precariously coherent self that faces these problems" (*RS*, 288 n. 9). Tillich may also be viewed as occupying a "transitional position," construing the human predicament in Oedipal terms, but portraying the self as struggling to manifest centeredness in spite of the pressures it experiences daily to allow itself to drift apart. Thus, in spite of his enmeshment in traditional Freudianism, Tillich sounded, at times, like the artists who spoke for the new age, as described here by Kohut:

> As contrasted with the central artistic challenge of our day, the art of yesterday—I am thinking especially of the great European novelists of the second half of the nineteenth and of the beginning of the twentieth century—dealt with the problems of Guilty Man—the man of the Oedipus complex, the man of structural conflict—who, strongly involved with his human environment from childhood on, is sorely tested by his wishes and desires. But the emotional problems of modern man are shifting, and the great modern artists were the first to respond in depth to man's new emotional task. Just as it is the understimulated child, the insufficiently responded-to child, the daughter deprived of an idealizable mother, the son deprived of an idealizable father, that has now become paradigmatic

for man's central problem in our Western world, so it is the crumbling, decomposing, fragmenting, enfeebled self of this child and, later, the fragile, vulnerable, empty self of the adult that the great artists of the day describe—through tone and word, on canvas and in stone—and that they try to heal. The musician of disordered sound, the poet of decomposed language, the painter and sculptor of the fragmented visual and tactile world: they all portray the breakup of the self and, through the reassemblage and rearrangement of the fragments, try to create new structures that possess wholeness, perfection, new meaning. (*RS*, 286)

Tillich's views on self-estrangement often have a similar tone, as when he praises Dante's *Divine Comedy* for its description of "the inner self-destructiveness of man in his estrangement from his essential being," and criticizes Zen Buddhism for its advocacy of a "formless self."[26] To illustrate and account for our self-estrangement, however, he invariably turns to the language and experience of guilt, and here we must part company with him, in spite of the fact that he is the one major theologian of the twentieth century who did not treat psychology—and psychologists—in a patronizing manner. For similar reasons, Kohut reluctantly but firmly parted company with Freud.

The Defensive Self

A second problematic that a theology of shame cannot afford to overlook is the defensive self, which leads those who have experienced shame to take steps to avoid additional shame experiences. By focusing on these defensive strategies, we can address a particularly vexing problem for a theology of shame that wants to take sin seriously, namely, how can we talk meaningfully about sin when those who experience shame are usually victims and have not done anything wrong? A theology of guilt does not have

26. Paul Tillich, *Theology of Culture*, ed. Robert C. Kimball (New York: Oxford Univ. Press, 1964), 123; James B. Ashbrook, "Paul Tillich Converses with Psychotherapists," in *MH*, 221.

this problem, because it focuses on wrongful or unjust actions for which the perpetrator may be held accountable. It makes perfect sense to call such actions sinful. In contrast, shame experiences are not wrongful in themselves. In fact, the very notion that the victim of a shame experience like incest or rape is partially responsible for the atrocity is thoroughly reprehensible. This is an illegitimate effort to turn a shame experience into a guilt experience, the fallacy into which Job's counselors fell.

The fact that one has been victimized in one's past is not, however, sufficient grounds for condoning wrongful actions by this same individual in the present and future. Even victims are accountable for their actions. Thus, Gershen Kaufman points out that persons who have experienced shame in their lives will often develop defensive strategies to enable them to avoid or blunt the painfulness of future experiences of shame.[27] These strategies enable us to identify characteristic ways in which shame victims succumb to actions and attitudes that may appropriately be labeled as sinful. The fact that our victimization was the cause of our resort to such defensive strategies is certainly an extenuating factor, but we must, at the same time, hold ourselves responsible for these defensive attitudes and actions. Not to do so is to take a fatalistic view of shame, as though shame permanently condemns us to a less than fully human existence in which we are held to be incapable of acting as a firm and cohesive self, a self that Kohut says has become "a center of initiative: a unit that tries to follow its own course" (RS, 245).

The defensive strategies identified by Kaufman include rage against others, contempt for others, striving for power, striving for perfection, transfer of blame, and internal withdrawal. Each of these strategies is potentially sinful, but we should pay particular attention to contempt for others, striving for power, and transfer of blame, all of which particularly concern personal accountability.

27. Gershen Kaufman, *Shame: The Power of Caring*, rev. ed. (Cambridge, Mass.: Schenkman Books, 1985), chap. 3.

In *contempt for others*, one externalizes shame by adopting a judgmental, faultfinding, or condescending attitude toward others. Holding others in contempt insulates the self against further shame, because contempt for others renders them incapable of daring to laugh at one. (This is very much like Bursten's paranoid type of narcissist.) In *power striving*, one gains control over situations so as to minimize the chances of further shaming. Such exercises of power may well include the shaming of others: "What, you haven't finished that report yet?" or "You are the most stupid person I've ever met!" In *transfer of blame*, one assigns the cause of shame to someone else by the familiar technique of scapegoating. Someone else, who usually cannot defend herself or himself, is accused of placing one in an embarrassing, humiliating, or shameful situation: "If you hadn't rushed me, I wouldn't have spilled the pitcher of juice!"

All three strategies deal with one's own shame by shaming someone else. Thus the victim of shame victimizes others. Sometimes the new victim is a member of one's own generation (often a spouse). Often, however, the victim is a defenseless child, and so the shaming process is passed from one generation to the next. Few children are sufficiently secure and perceptive enough to realize that they are being shamed because their parents cannot tolerate their own shame. All three defensive strategies introduce serious distortion into human relationships, and in this way shame not only reflects our sinful condition, but also becomes the cause of sinful behavior against others. Furthermore, these defensive strategies, precisely because they insulate us from our own experience of shame, are the cause of self-estrangement—we isolate ourselves from our own shameful self. The shame experience is not embraced as our own experience, and therefore as integral to the self, but is denied, protected against, and projected onto others. It is "embraced," then, only as the experience of others. They are shamed, while our own involvement in shame is vigorously denied.

Much more could be said about these defensive strategies and their implications for a Christian understanding of sin. But the point here is simply to draw attention to these strategies as a means of addressing the predictable charge that a theology of shame is likely to be soft on the issue of personal culpability. Our experience of victimization makes us deeply aware of the sinful condition in which all humanity is implicated, but how we react to this experience is also of crucial importance; it is possible— indeed, likely—that we will respond in ways that are destructive to self and others. Ourselves the victims of shame, we are disposed to victimize others, especially those who are weak and vulnerable, who are unable to defend themselves against these assaults on their own vital selves. Augustine, for example, subjected his illegitimate son to the same shaming techniques to which he had been subjected when he was a child.[28]

The Depleted Self

A third problematic that a theology of shame needs to take se-riously is the depleted self, the term that Kohut uses to describe the long-term effects of shaming. For Kohut, self-depletion is a less severe form of self-pathology than self-fragmentation, or the disintegration of the self, but it is, for that very reason, a far more common experience, and is found among those who appear to be leading productive lives. Kohut observed such self-depletion in patients who described "subtly experienced, yet pervasive feel-ings of emptiness and depression" (AS, 16). Such patients had the impression that they were not fully real, or at least that their emotions were dulled; they were doing their work without zest, seeking routines to carry them along because they lacked initia-tive. Kohut contends: "These and many other similar complaints are indicative of the ego's depletion because it has to wall itself off against the unrealistic claims of an archaic grandiose self, or against the intense hunger for a powerful external supplier of self-esteem and other forms of emotional sustenance in the nar-cissistic realm" (AS, 17). For Kohut, the connecting link between shame and self-depletion is "the dejection of defeat," the failure to achieve one's nuclear ambitions and ideals, and the realization

28. See Capps, "Augustine's *Confessions*," 69–92.

that one cannot remedy the failure in the time and with the energies still at one's disposal. Kohut calls this a "nameless shame," a "guiltless despair," and says that it is most commonly found among persons in late middle age, though it is certainly not exclusive to them (*RS*, 238, 241).

The experience of depletion is to a theology of shame what anxiety was, and continues to be, to a theology of guilt. Tillich defined anxiety as "the awareness of that element of non-being (of the negation of what one is) which is identical with finitude, the coming from nothing and the going toward nothing" (WBHN, 190). He contended that the feeling of guilt intensifies anxiety because it adds to the natural awareness that one must eventually die, an anxiety that it would not have without guilt, namely, the feeling of standing under judgment. Anxiety in this case is the response to the judgment, both from without and from within, that one has misused freedom.

Without rejecting the validity of Tillich's analysis of guilt and anxiety, a theology of shame will inevitably place greater emphasis on self-failures than misuses of human freedom. It will not use the language of anxiety, but of depletion, and will talk, as Kohut does, about our nameless shame, our guiltless despair, our sense of mortification for having failed to live lives of significance and meaning. For Tillich, the challenge is to live courageously, to use one's freedom in full awareness that, in using it, one will also misuse it. For a theology of shame, the challenge is to live with failure. This challenge is most deeply felt among those whose lives are outwardly successful, for, as Kohut points out, these persons are succeeding to a degree in meeting the unrealistic claims of an archaic grandiose self, and are therefore most vulnerable to the "nameless shame" that accompanies the realization that one is nonetheless failing.

Tillich says that, in the story of Gethsemane, Jesus was "grasped by a profound anxiety about his having to suffer and to die—an anxiety which is neither neurotic nor connected with guilt, but which is the natural expression of everything finite when anticipating the partial negation of suffering and the total negation of death" (WBHN, 190). A theology of shame will not focus on a quality that marked Christ's radical difference from us—his guilt-lessness—but on an experience he shared with us: the sense of failure, the dejection of defeat, and the realization that one cannot remedy the failure. This is the deepest meaning of Gethsemane from the perspective of a theology of shame. The story of the cross is the story of the depleted self. For Jesus, it was not primarily the public humiliation that made this a shameful event, but the inner awareness, the self-realization, that, from his own perspective, his life had failed.

Kohut assures us that his patients do not always, or persistently, experience themselves as depleted. Nor do they believe that the word "failure" is an adequate description of their lives, for, after all, they have had many successes in life and can point to many achievements. Nor is their mood or temperament continually one of depression or of lethargy, for there are times when they feel elation and inner vitality. Kohut is not, therefore, necessarily speaking of a personality trait or a dominant life attitude. The issue is not pessimism, for it is possible to maintain an optimistic view of life and frame of mind and still experience oneself as depleted. Instead, Kohut is speaking of "subtle experiences" of self-depletion that may occur without one being aware of them, but that, cumulatively, wear down and diminish the vital, living self. He is identifying the deeper and more subtle effects of shame upon one's life. The words that capture this deeper, inner experience of shame are not humiliation and embarrassment, but words like empty, exhausted, drained, demoralized, depressed, deflated, bereft, needy, starving, apathetic, passive, and weak. If humiliation and embarrassment are good words for describing the feature of shame that *can* be named, depletion and its various synonyms capture the "nameless shame," the shame that is often too deep and too demoralizing for words.

These depletion words are commonly used in the traditional literature on the deadly sins to describe the sin of apathy, or *acedia*. So perhaps one can say that as theologies of guilt focus on the sin of pride, here viewed as the inflated sense of self that leads to the misuse of human freedom, a theology of shame centers on the sin of apathy, and explores the manner in which the Christian tradition has supported, but also frustrated, the work of self-repair.[29]

These three are not the only problematics of the self that shame experiences reveal to us, nor are these problematics revealed to us only through experiences of shame. But by focusing on shame we become aware of problematics of the self, and thus of fundamental truths about ourselves, that a theology of guilt may well ignore or obscure.

If theology is to be a resource of healing, it needs to center, as we have done here, on the problematics of the self. This, however, is only one part of its role, for theology, if it is to function as therapeutic wisdom, needs also to address the "therapeutics of the self," that is, the question of what it would mean for us to experience wholeness. As William James writes at the beginning of his chapter in *The Varieties of Religious Experience* on conversion:

> To be converted, to be regenerated, to receive grace, to experience religion, to gain an assurance, are so many phrases which denote the process, gradual or sudden, by which a self hitherto divided, and consciously wrong, inferior and unhappy, becomes unified and consciously right, superior and happy, in consequence of its firmer hold upon religious realities.[30]

The "therapeutics of the self" will be addressed in the final chapter, thus completing our formulation of a theology of shame. Intervening chapters address the common argument that the root cause of narcissism is individualism, and the cure is therefore some form of genuine community. This popular diagnosis needs critical assessment. Especially we need to ask: Does it take sufficient account of the role played by social institutions in creating conditions for the emergence of the narcissistic self in our day and time?

29. See Mary Louise Bringle, *Despair: Sickness or Sin?* (Nashville: Abingdon, 1990), for a theological analysis of *acedia*.
30. James, *The Varieties of Religious Experience*, 157.

5

Expressive Individualism as Scapegoat

*W*hen societies realize that something is terribly wrong with them—that they have become something very different from what they were originally envisioned to be—many resort to the strategy of scapegoating. They either identify one segment of the society as the cause of the problem and see that these persons are eliminated through execution or exile, or they sacrifice an obviously innocent member or members of the society (usually a child) to expiate the society's guilt and to put moral force behind its vow to repent.

In *Job, The Victim of His People,* René Girard notes that the scapegoat is often the victim of physical violence. However, there are instances when violent language instead is employed against the victim. The harshness of Job's counselors is often attributed to their awkwardness and to the strictness of their theology, and the sheer violence of their verbal attack on him is overlooked. Comparing these verbal attacks to the actions of a lynching mob, Girard points out:

Words, too, form a crowd; countless, they swirl about the head of the victim, gathering to deliver the *coup de grâce*. The three series of speeches are like volleys of arrows aimed at the enemy of God. The accusations descend on Job like so many adversaries, intent upon the destruction of some friend. Their hostile speeches are not merely an image of collective violence, they are a form of active participation in it. Job is well aware of this, and denounces the verbal dismemberment to which he is subjected. The three friends crush him with their speeches, and pulverize him with words (19:2).[1]

Maseo Yamaguchi points out that the scapegoat subject to verbal denunciation is not always a human person. In the academic world, a scientific theory, a philosophical world view, or a school of thought may become the object of the scapegoating mechanism:

Human beings are less rational than they like to believe. They make decisions more on the basis of hidden fear than on rational grounds. We are all afraid of being rejected by the community formed around a collective decision, and of being left behind, as can be seen in the realm of fashion. It is natural to take the side of the scapegoat-makers rather than that of the scapegoat itself. So too the history of any science will show that the prevailing academic theory suddenly passes into the background, seeming to lose its power of attraction. . . . Scientists thus lean towards the fashionable side. They are afraid of being identified with what is believed to be becoming obsolescent and willingly participate in the effort to reject the outdated theory.[2]

In recent years, scapegoating through verbal attack has occurred in the seemingly rational sociological and theological analyses of what is wrong with American society. Individualism, especially in its expressive form, has been identified as the major

1. René Girard, *Job: The Victim of His People*, trans. Yvonne Freccero (Stanford, Calif.: Stanford Univ. Press, 1987), 26.
2. Maseo Yamaguchi, "Towards a Poetics of the Scapegoat," in *Violence and Truth: On the Work of René Girard*, ed. Paul Dumouchel (Stanford, Calif.: Stanford Univ. Press, 1988), 183.

reason why our society is not what we have envisioned it to be. The aspect of this scapegoating of individualism that applies here is the condemnation of individualism for its alleged role in creating the social conditions within which narcissism has taken root and flourished.

In the theological community, the most prevalent explanation for the emergence of narcissism in our time is that we, as a society, have succumbed to the allures of individualism, that is, everyone acts out of his or her own self-interest and does not consider the needs and aspirations of others. What those who take this position have failed to explain, however, is how individualism has done this. What is the social process or mechanism through which individualism has given rise to narcissism?

Others in the theological community have talked as though narcissism and individualism were synonymous. They use the two words interchangeably, or in tandem; they refer to the "individualistic and narcissistic age" in which we live. The implication is that both terms—"individualism" and "narcissism"—say essentially the same thing, usually meaning that we live in an age of selfishness and self-centeredness, an age in which too many of us place our own interests first, and are willing to do almost anything to get what we want regardless of the consequences to others. Those who adopt this position, however, ignore the fact that individualism is an ideology while narcissism is a psychological condition.

Instead of assuming that individualism is either the cause of narcissism or synonymous with it, we would do well to explore their relationship in a more objective fashion. To do so, we need to take a closer look at what is currently being said about individualism, focusing on the discussion initiated by the authors of the best-selling book, *Habits of the Heart*.[3]

3. Robert N. Bellah et al., *Habits of the Heart: Individualism and Commitment in American Life* (Berkeley: Univ. of California Press, 1985).

The Attack on Expressive Individualism

In *Habits of the Heart*, Robert Bellah and his coauthors provide these definitions of individualism: (1) a belief in the inherent dignity and, indeed, sacredness of the human person; and (2) a belief that the individual has a primary reality whereas society is a second-order, derived or artificial construct, a view they call *ontological individualism* (*HH*, 334). They contrast ontological individualism with their own position, *social realism*, which views "society as a reality in itself" and "not as something merely derived from the agreement of individuals" (*HH*, 303).

In the preface of *Habits of the Heart*, Bellah and his colleagues draw attention to Alexis de Tocqueville's warning in the 1830s that "some aspects of our character—what he was one of the first to call 'individualism'—might eventually isolate Americans one from another, and thereby undermine the conditions of freedom" (*HH*, vii). Viewing Tocqueville as prophetic, Bellah and his colleagues are concerned "that this individualism may have grown cancerous—that it may be destroying those social integuments that Tocqueville saw as moderating its more destructive potentialities, that it may be threatening the survival of freedom itself" (*HH*, vii).

Especially destructive, according to them, is the expressive form of individualism, which they trace historically to the New England Transcendentalists, especially Emerson and Thoreau, with Walt Whitman representing expressive individualism in its clearest form. In their view, the other form of individualism—utilitarian individualism—had good intentions. Benjamin Franklin, its originator, understood that only a certain kind of society was likely to accord the ordinary citizen the right to be treated with dignity and respect. He devoted his life to bringing into being a society that would secure the individual rights of its citizens, and would, in turn, enable them to set themselves to the work of self-improvement: "But for many of those influenced by Franklin, the focus was so exclusively on individual self-improvement that the larger social context hardly came into view.

By the end of the eighteenth century, there would be those who would argue that in a society where each vigorously pursued his own interest, the social good would automatically emerge. This would be utilitarian individualism in pure form" (*HH*, 33).

Expressive individualism, however, is attacked more vigorously by Bellah and his colleagues because they believe it is the dominant form of individualism in our own era. Arguing that expressive individualism is essentially a celebration of the self, that it has little to do with material acquisition (as utilitarian individualism does), but almost everything to do with "the freedom to express oneself, against all constraints and conventions" (*HH*, 34), they contend that the dangers of expressive individualism have become all-too-clear with the emergence of the "therapeutic ethos." This ethos "is suggestive of these [difficulties] because it is the way in which contemporary Americans live out the tenets of modern individualism. For psychology, as Robert Coles has written, the self is 'the only or main form of reality' " (*HH*, 143).

Thus, whereas utilitarian individualism focuses on self-improvement, especially through material resources, expressive individualism centers on self-expression. For Bellah and his colleagues, the bankruptcy of expressive individualism is glaringly apparent in its cult of self-worship. The authors go somewhat easy on Whitman, in part because he shared Franklin's ideal of the self-sufficient farmer or artisan who is capable of participation in the common life. But elsewhere Bellah comes down very hard against Emerson for inflating the self until it is identical with Universal being, and speaking derisively against the notion that we should depend on one another.[4] According to Bellah, in expressing such views, Emerson rejects "the normative authority of the New Testament" and reveals his true colors, that is, "his intention to deliver a comparable revelation for his own day."[5]

4. Robert N. Bellah, "The Quest for the Self: Individualism, Morality, Politics," in Paul Rabinow and William M. Sullivan, eds., *Interpretive Social Science: A Second Look* (Berkeley: Univ. of California Press, 1987), 365–83.
5. Ibid., 368.

The theological community has joined the attack on individualism. Some, like John Cobb, are more concerned about the effects of utilitarian individualism. He argues that the modern economy "works against human community because it is based on a radically individualistic view of human beings. Because what is valued is not community, but only per capita consumption of goods and services, community is destroyed whenever it stands in the way of increasing the total quantity of goods and services." He contends that the political, economic, and cultural individualism of the Enlightenment was rooted "in a physical and metaphysical individualism which has also proved inadequate and misleading. Modern science thought of the world as composed of indivisible units—atoms—which related to each other only externally. Their relative spatial locations could change, but this change had no internal effect on them. An atom remained self-identical and unchanged forever!" For Cobb, the answer is found in a new appreciation for the good of the community. As we humans are internally related to one another, "We can improve human welfare, accordingly, only as we build and improve communities."[6]

C. Ellis Nelson is more concerned with expressive individualism. Citing *Habits of the Heart*, he repeats Tocqueville's warning that individualism might eventually isolate Americans from one another and thereby undermine the conditions of freedom: "In other words, if democracy became only a process by which individuals obtained rights, then anything is approved that can be achieved by majority vote. But American democracy was built on substantial social values, such as a concern for fairness, a regard for the rights of others, and a willingness to use one's own time and abilities for the welfare of the community. These social values are the necessary characteristics of our culture before a democratic political order can provide individual rights."[7] In Nelson's judgment, individualism undermines such values, and one

6. John B. Cobb, Jr., "From Individualism to Persons in Community: A Postmodern Economic Theory," in David Ray Griffin, ed., *Sacred Interconnections: Postmodern Spirituality, Political Economy, and Art* (Albany: State Univ. of New York Press, 1990), 123–42.
7. C. Ellis Nelson, *How Faith Matures* (Louisville: Westminster/John Knox Press, 1989), 39.

of its consequences is the privatization of religion that is so evident today:

> Authority is not in God, who comes into a person's life with a mission; it is rooted in a person's psychological needs. Although these needs may not be conscious desires, they exert enough pressure to make people choose a religion that feeds them. The search is not for truth about God but for religious beliefs and practices that help people cope with inner difficulties or provide a way to make sense out of the variety of events taking place around them. Seeing many options, including a half dozen or more on television, people select what fits their needs. Under these circumstances religion is secular in that it is used for self-fulfillment.[8]

Nelson notes the contemporary "shift away from the corporate aspect of religion. Until recent times Protestants had considerable loyalty to their denomination and a sense of accountability to a congregation. In the place of this loyalty has emerged the idea of a congregation as an assembly of like-minded individuals seeking personal satisfactions."[9]

In a collection of essays entitled *Beyond Individualism*, Donald Gelpi praises the authors of *Habits of the Heart* for having addressed "the morally corrosive potential latent in American individualism" and for noting that "individualism repeatedly betrays the consciences of well-meaning Americans into one moral impasse after another." As an ideology it presents "contemporary Americans with false and destructive options in almost every area of their lives: in religion, in married life, in the therapeutic search for emotional integration, and in the political search for the common good."[10] Gelpi also agrees with the proposals in *Habits* for doing something about individualism, namely, "a systematic

8. Ibid., 38.
9. Ibid., 39.
10. Donald L. Gelpi, ed., *Beyond Individualism: Toward a Retrieval of Moral Discourse in America* (Notre Dame, Ind.: Univ. of Notre Dame Press, 1989), 3.

retrieval of our religious heritage as a nation and of the republican strain in our political philosophy, which better reconciles concern for individual rights and the common good than does either utilitarian or expressive individualism."[11]

Gelpi also shares Bellah's antipathy for Emerson; he says that Emerson "functioned as the self-appointed prophet of this new romantic ethos and found enthusiastic disciples in Henry David Thoreau, Walt Whitman, and scores of American youth." What did he proclaim to these impressionable youths? According to Gelpi, he affirmed that "at the heart of each person lies a unique core of intuition and feeling that demands creative expression and needs protection against the encroachments both of other individuals and of social institutions." He also said that those "who fritter away their personal creative potential allegedly sacrifice their real personal identity to unthinking social conformity, that perennial 'hobgoblin of little minds.' "[12]

What Emerson actually said in his essay "Self-Reliance," delivered not to an audience of "impressionable youths" but to adults of all ages, is that "a foolish consistency is the hobgoblin of small, little minds, adored by little statesmen, and philosophers and divines." He made reference in this passage not to social conformity but to the habit of these "small, little minds" to become slaves to their theories. For example, they will hold to their metaphysical theories that deny personality to the Deity even though they have themselves experienced God in their own souls as a living being. When faced with such a discrepancy between theory and experience, they defer to their theories. For Emerson, this is very wrong. Instead, "Leave your theory as Joseph [left] his coat in the hand of the harlot, and flee" (SR, 33). Gelpi's misreading of Emerson here suggests that he is more interested in scapegoating expressive individualism than in listening to what Emerson has to say. Still, he is right to point out that Emerson was a vigorous opponent of "social conformity," not, however,

11. Ibid.
12. Gelpi, "Conversion: Beyond the Impasses of Individualism," in Gelpi, ed., *Beyond Individualism*, 2.

because he was a proponent of the rights of individuals to absolute self-expression, but because he believed individuals should submit to the sterner claims and standards that one places upon oneself, and that enable one "to dispense with the popular code." He added, "If any one imagines that this law is lax, let him keep its commandment one day" (SR, 42).

Since the theologians' attack on expressive individualism was fomented by *Habits*, we need to take a closer look at the way Bellah et al. have depicted expressive individualism, and compare this to what Emerson actually taught.

The Isolated Self

A persistent theme of *Habits of the Heart* is that expressive individualism is inherently isolationist, celebrating the lone individual. Bellah illustrates these allegedly isolative tendencies of individualism by associating it with two cultural hero types, the cowboy and the detective (*HH*, 144–46). While they also cite Abraham Lincoln as an individualist who identified deeply with a community and a tradition, their choice of the cowboy and detective to illustrate individualism supports the claim being made here that they and their supporters are engaging in verbal scapegoating. Emerson would not have devoted so much attention to the problem of social conformity, especially its destructive effects on one's inner character, if he did not assume that the individual would be an active participant in social life. As Yehoshua Arieli points out, Emerson believed that our fundamental need is to regain selfhood, "to rediscover and habituate ourselves to our lost souls," and this could only be achieved by breaking through social conventions, creeds, institutions, and personal and social habit.[13] But regaining one's selfhood is not achieved by escaping society or becoming antisocial. Indeed, in "Self-Reliance," he inveighs against educated Americans' penchant for

13. Yehoshua Arieli, *Individualism and Nationalism in American Ideology* (Cambridge: Harvard Univ. Press, 1964), 277.

travel, for in traveling, one "travels away from himself." Furthermore, "the rage of travelling is a symptom of a deeper unsoundness affecting the whole intellectual action. The intellect is vagabond, and our system of education fosters restlessness" (SR, 46–47). If Emerson feels so strongly about travel to other countries, it is inconceivable that he would praise, much less celebrate, the life of the lonely cowboy and the socially alienated detective.

In "The Quest for the Self," Bellah does not say that Emerson's "true self" is entirely antisocial, but he contends that Emerson's norms for human association are a contractual model of human relationships unformed by convention and tradition, and an "expressive" model of connectedness in relationships that transcend convention and tradition. Both models "depend on the absolutely autonomous wills of the individuals involved," and neither envision "any objective normative order governing the relationship, any transcendent loyalty above the wishes of the individuals involved, any community that is really there independent of the wills of the individuals who compose it."[14] Here Bellah is critiquing Emerson's individualism from the perspective of the ideology of social realism.

Emerson's response to this criticism is twofold. First, he simply disagrees with the social realist position. In "Self-Reliance" he observes that "Society is a wave. The wave moves onward, but the water of which it is composed, does not. The same particle does not rise from the valley to the ridge. Its unity is only phenomenal" (SR, 49). Moreover, "Society never advances. It recedes as fast on one side as it gains on the other. For everything that is given, some is taken. Society acquires new arts and loses old instincts" (SR, 48). This disagreement with the social realist position is no mere philosophical argument for him, but arises from a spiritual and moral concern that individuals have looked away from themselves and toward society for so long, focusing their attention on religious, learned and civil institutions, that they no longer have much self-esteem, and take no real pride in their own

14. Bellah, "The Quest for the Self," in *Interpretive Social Science*, Rabinow and Sullivan, eds., 373.

actions: "We let society choose for us, and if we miscarry in our first enterprises, we lose heart, and allow society to declare us ruined" (SR, 43). We also participate in our own self-diminishment by our willing acquiescence to ideologies that affirm the priority of society over the individual. Such acquiescence eventually produces self-hatred when individuals realize that they have allowed mere theories to rob them of their one and only life on earth. No social theory, however compelling, and no social institution, however worthy, warrants such an ultimate self-sacrifice.

Second, it is true that Emerson makes a plea for a certain degree of solitariness: "I like the silent church before the service begins, better than any preaching" (SR, 41). But he pleads for solitariness so that we may have real community, without the debilitating effects of "lying hospitality and lying affection" (SR, 41). Through greater trust in ourselves achieved through intentional acts of self-reflection (similar to prayer), we will effect a "revolution" in human relations and in the ways that we associate with one another. The deepening and strengthening of our true selfhood will result in more satisfying, more authentic human associations, expressive of the real convictions and desires of those who come together. Absolute independence results in loneliness, but individuals are even more desperately lonely when they are compelled to misrepresent themselves, to put forth a false self.

Communities of Memory

Another major theme in *Habits of the Heart* is the opposition of expressive individualism to communities of memory, that is, groups of people who are socially interdependent, who participate together in discussion and decision making, who share certain practices, and who recognize that the group is shaped in part by its past and its memory of its past (*HH*, 333). Expressive individualists are not necessarily hostile or antagonistic to communities of memory, but they speak a very different language. The "language of the self-reliant individual is the first language of

American moral life" while "the languages of tradition and commitment in communities of memory are 'second languages' that most Americans know as well, and which they use when the language of the radically separate self does not seem adequate" (*HH*, 154).

In "The Quest for the Self," Bellah examines Emerson's plea for individuals to become the self they truly are, and claims that what this has come to mean today is that individuals see their true selves as that which remains after their pasts, the social situations that have previously enveloped them, and the obligations and constraints imposed by others, have been stripped away. The "true self" in this view is the unentailed self, the self who is radically autonomous of other selves, and essentially without a history. In his view, such a self is improvisational and ultimately empty.[15] In *Habits*, the authors note that such an "empty self" is "an analytic concept, a limit toward which we tend, but not a concrete reality" (*HH*, 154). Still, to the extent that the self is improvisational and empty, expressive individualism is largely to blame. Since churches are among our most prominent and cherished communities of memory, the conflict between expressive individualism and our religious communities is clear. This is the point of C. Ellis Nelson's critique of expressive individualism.

For Emerson, however, the blame for this conflict lies not with individualism but with the churches, which have substituted formalism for the living spirit of religion. In his "Divinity School Address," he contends that the churches have caused individuals to doubt themselves, to subordinate their own intuitions and convictions to the views of those who are more powerful than they, and to mistrust their own experience when it conflicts with church teachings. The churches have also subverted the intention of Jesus himself that each of us reflect the God that is in us, and not live our lives in deference to or imitation of another.[16]

15. Ibid., 372.
16. Ralph Waldo Emerson, "Divinity School Address," in *Emerson: Essays and Lectures* (New York: The Library of America, 1983), 73–92.

He also warns against the worship of the past. In "Self-Reliance," he warns:

> If . . . a man claims to know and speak of God, and carries you backward to the phraseology of some old mouldered nation in another country, in another world, believe him not. Is the acorn better than the oak which is its fulness and completion? Is the parent better than the child into whom he has cast his ripened being? (SR, 38).

If Bellah talks about communities of memory and of hope, Emerson is concerned with living fully and unapologetically in the now. He contrasts humans with the roses under his window. These roses

> make no reference to former roses or to better ones; they are for what they are; they exist with God today. . . . But man postpones or remembers; he does not live in the present, but with reverted eye laments the past, or, heedless of the riches that surround him, stands on tiptoe to foresee the future. He cannot be happy and strong until he too lives with nature in the present, above time. (SR, 38–39)

Yet, if he does not have many positive things to say about the church in its role of community of memory, there are two brief paragraphs at the end of the Divinity School Address that offer encouragement to those about to embark on careers in ministry. Rejecting the attempt to project and establish a new religious system, he calls on his listeners to let the breath of new life "be breathed by you through the forms already existing. For, if once you are alive, you shall find they still become plastic and new. The remedy to deformity is, first, soul, and second, soul, and evermore, soul."[17] Two forms that Christianity makes available today—the Sabbath, with its celebration of the dignity of spiritual being—and the institution of preaching, with the opportunities

17. Ibid., 91.

it affords to speak the truth and to cheer fainting hearts—are available to address this deformity, and it is for each individual to make of them what he or she can and will. There is nothing inherently wrong with memory, but all too often we remember for the purpose of imitating those forms and persons who have gone before us. We say that we recall the past so that we will not be doomed to repeat it, but the very opposite occurs. Remembering the past, we repeat it. Hope comes from knowing that we are free to be original, that we need follow no model or form, but may be the self that we uniquely and truly are. While this sounds like the proverbial "self-made" man or woman, it is much more than this. We have been bequeathed a soul that is not of our own making, but is the very spirit of God within us. If we are unaccustomed to viewing ourselves as having divinity in us, this is because we have denied common humanity while ascribing divinity to Jesus. The very antithesis of the self-made, we are a divine creation, the very soul of God. He longs for the day when the world itself becomes "the mirror of the soul."[18]

Emerson is arguing, therefore, that expressive individualists like himself did not declare war on the churches—the communities of memory—but rather found that the churches were inhospitable to those whose most urgent and pressing spiritual need was to regain selfhood, to discover or rediscover grounds for self-trust: "Trust thyself: every heart vibrates to that iron string" (SR, 28). Key to such self-recovery is the individual's natural affinity to the soul of God, which underwrites our inner trust and confidence. Evidence that the churches continue in their inhospitality to such endangered souls are these words of C. Ellis Nelson:

> Authority is not in God, who comes into a person's life with a mission; it is rooted in a person's psychological needs. . . . The search is not for truth about God but for religious beliefs and practices that help people cope with inner difficulties or provide a way to make sense out of the variety of events taking place around them.

18. Ibid., 92.

What is so wrong with churches helping people cope with in, difficulties and make sense of events taking place around them? And why assume that divine authority and human mission is incommensurate with our psychological needs?

Fragile and Threatening?

Yamaguchi identifies a curious paradox in scapegoating: Why is it, he asks, that those who are engaged in the scapegoating believe their victim is so powerful? If it is relatively easy for them to attack their victim, and so difficult for the victim to counter-attack, one would think that they would view their victim as powerless. But they do not. Yamaguchi suggests that this paradox is probably due to the fact that, while the victim is weak in social terms, on a symbolic level, the victim has a potentially very great power of provocation. Usually, the victim is unaware of having such power.[19]

In his afterword to the Gelpi volume, Bellah acknowledges that he and his coauthors may have been too hard on expressive individualism. He notes, for example, that they had downplayed the fact that some individuals, experiencing the available "communities of memory" as narrow and oppressive, and yet unwilling to take the route of utilitarian individualism, have "attempted through some version of expressive individualism to find a new way." He adds, "It is true that in *Habits* we do not take seriously enough this phenomenon." Some consideration was in fact given to it, he claims, in the chapter on religion, "where we argue that religious individualism, a form of expressive individualism, presents a serious challenge to the established churches and sects. We indicate there the institutional fragility of religious individualism, and the same is true of expressive individualism generally, yet we take it seriously as a social phenomenon. But we should have made the point more generally and thus been fairer to the culturally positive possibilities in expressive individualism."[20]

19. Yamaguchi, "Towards a Poetics," in *Violence and Truth*, ed. Dumouchel, 186.
20. Bellah, in *Beyond Individualism*, ed. Gelpi, 221.

If, however, expressive individualism has been so fragile from an institutional standpoint, why do Bellah et al. view it as so threatening? It would seem from this admission of theirs that the institutions have been quite successful in fending it off. That it has never had much influence, especially in *religious* institutions, is suggested in their chapter on religion. Referring to religious individualists like Jefferson and Paine, they note: "Many of the most influential figures in nineteenth-century American culture could find a home in none of the existing religious bodies, though they were attracted to the religious teachings of several traditions. One thinks of Ralph Waldo Emerson, Henry David Thoreau, and Walt Whitman." Furthermore, in spite of the fact that "religious bodies had to compete in a consumers' market and grew or declined in terms of changing patterns of individual religious taste, . . . religious individualism in the United States could not be contained within the churches, however diverse they were" (*HH*, 233).

The obvious conclusion to draw from these observations, but one which Bellah et al. do not acknowledge, is that the churches, while becoming more diverse and more responsive to changing patterns of individual religious taste, were united in their lack of sympathy for religious (e.g., Emersonian) individualism and in their determination to see that it did not gain a foothold in any of the churches. Otherwise, its proponents may have found a "home" in the existing religious bodies, and their views would have gained a hearing there. If Bellah is now prepared to acknowledge that what happened in the religious institutions applies "more generally" to American society as a whole, this is, in substance, an admission that individualism has been effectively screened out and excluded from American social institutions. Thus, with regard to social institutions, individualism is not just, as Emerson once lamented, "an experiment that has never been tried,"[21] but a school of thought that has been forcefully and systematically excluded.

21. See Arieli, *Individualism*, 277.

No wonder, then, that religious individualism, especially in its expressive form, suffers from "institutional fragility." The religious institutions, then and now, have little use for it. Lacking an institutional location, expressive individualism was driven into "culture." While Bellah is now prepared to accept the proposition that there are some "culturally positive possibilities in expressive individualism," he does not say what these might be.

It is difficult to comprehend how it is possible to claim that individualism is such a threat to American society while acknowledging that it has failed to make significant inroads in American institutional life. Bellah's own analysis of the situation, with religion serving as his test case, suggests that individualism is not the threat that he and his coauthors claim it to be. After all, they acknowledge that the churches succeeded in driving it out, and they do not claim that other institutions were any less successful. If institutionalization is the evidence of an ideology's real power in a society (a reasonably safe assumption), then, by their own analysis, individualism is not much of a threat. Expressive individualism is not the voice of the triumphant, but, to borrow Karl Marx's poignant description of religion, it is "the sigh of the oppressed creature,"[22] of the beleaguered, depleted self.

"The Uphill Battle"

On the other hand, Bellah argues that, whereas the nineteenth century was more successful in keeping expressive individualism out of the churches, we in the late twentieth century are allowing it to gain an entrance. This is what C. Ellis Nelson also sees happening. In buying into the therapeutic ethos, the churches in our day are allowing expressive individualism to establish a foothold in our religious institutions, and the effect of this has been

22. Karl Marx, *On Religion: Karl Marx and Friedrich Engels* (New York: Schocken Books, 1974), 42. The full quotation reads, "Religion is the sigh of the oppressed creature, the heart of a heartless world, just as it is the spirit of a spiritless situation. It is the opium of the people."

the weakening of the churches, for individualism challenges a fundamental tenet of the churches' own self-understanding, namely, that the church "has a temporal and even ontological priority over the individual" (*HH*, 243).

In their case illustrations in their chapter on religion, Bellah makes the point that not only laity but also clergy have bought into ontological individualism (i.e., belief in the primary reality of individuals over society), and that clergy who resist this trend are fighting an uphill battle. This from an interview with an Episcopal priest:

> When asked whether his parishioners view the church as a necessary condition of their faith or as an organization that is optional for the Christian, the rector replied, "it's a constant uphill battle." He finds that contemporary American life "places enormous pressures on people to marginalize and isolate them and force them away from community," pressures that run absolutely contrary to the biblical understanding of life. When people can genuinely "hear scripture" and "experience community," he says, they realize that the church is a necessity, not an option. Concomitantly, Father Morrison finds that the idea of valid authority does not come easily: "The concept that a community can set standards, adopt values, capture conscience, and become authoritative in the life of human beings is not obvious in our culture, and it falls apart without it." When individuation is more important than community, "people are not together enough to take on the responsibilities of authority." (*HH*, 240–41)

The people, then, seem to adhere to a kind of ontological individualism, and the problems with this are reflected in the fact that they do not put much stock in community-established standards, or allow a community to "become authoritative" in their lives. Yet, while Father Morrison believes that our society "falls apart" without such community standards and authority, the authors point out that, "although the Episcopal church relaxed its absolute prohibition of divorce over twenty-five years ago, Father Morrison finds that marriage is currently in high esteem" (*HH*,

240–41). Apparently, these Episcopalians have found that what Emerson says is true, namely, that the claims and standards that one places upon oneself are "sterner" than those of the popular code.

Also, Father Morrison's parishioners objected to his tendency "to assume that Christian commitment meant taking some organizational or committee responsibility within the parish. 'They said,' he reports, 'we are in difficult places in the world and we think we should be here. Support us where we are. That was their criticism of me, which I took very much to heart.' He finds that 'strong lay people' are 'working in banks, in corporations, or at the university where they find it is very difficult to live out the Christian life and they're very lonely and they musn't be' " (*HH*, 241).

What, then, is Father Morrison up against? What is his fight, his "constant uphill battle," directed against? His parishioners do subscribe to an ontological individualism, where they assume that they, as individuals, are more real than society. Yet, while the Episcopal church has relaxed its official position on divorce, Father Morrison's parishioners are taking marriage more, not less, seriously than ever. Also, their reluctance to have their Christian faith equated with their involvement in organizational responsibilities within the parish reflects their desire for the church to be something other than the mirror image of institutions for which they work during the week. To his credit, Father Morrison has taken their objections seriously, has heard the sigh of the oppressed and lonely creature, and has promised that he will do everything in his power to keep the church from becoming an institution just like those they experience during the week.

But where does this leave Bellah et al. and their view that individualism is the source of Father Morrison's difficulties? Individualism, especially in its expressive form, is the catalyst behind these parishioners' commitment to real community, as exemplified in the fact that these individualists value marriage more highly (in spite of ecclesiastical standards being lowered), and they want to relate to one another in informal, nonorganizational ways.

It is unfortunate, therefore, that the effect of *Habits'* popularity within theological communities is that individualism has been identified as a serious and formidable threat to community. The lack or loss of community, not to mention the loneliness and inner depletion of individuals, is rarely attributed to the modern organizational structures from which Father Morrison's parishioners were trying to escape on Sunday morning. Even in their more recent book, *The Good Society,* the authors have virtually nothing to say about the fact that, as Father Morrison himself observed, it is our social institutions that make individuals feel lonely.[23]

Bellah and his colleagues point out that they have nothing against individuality as such, that their argument is with individualism. For them the "church idea" (i.e., the view that the church has ontological priority over the individual) affirms individuality, but individuality within community. Thus,

> the great contribution that the church idea can make today is its emphasis on the fact that individuality and society are not opposites but require each other. It was perhaps necessary at a certain stage in the development of modern society for individuals to declare their independence from churches, states, and families. But absolute independence becomes the atomism Tocqueville feared, a condition for a new despotism worse than the old. The church idea reminds us that in our independence we count on others and helps us to see that a healthy, grown-up independence is one that admits to healthy, grown-up dependence on others. Absolute independence is a false ideal. It delivers not the autonomy it promises but loneliness and vulnerability instead. (*HH,* 247)

However, this affirmation of individuality while denouncing individualism perpetuates the false idea that expressive individualism affirms the "absolute independence" of the individual. Also, the very fact that Bellah claims that the biblical tradition

---

23. Robert N. Bellah et al., *The Good Society* (New York: Alfred A. Knopf, 1991).

supports social realism against ontological individualism implies that the religious individualists' understanding of the Christian faith is inferior to that of the social realists. Even Bellah's adoption of a tone of resignation (i.e., acknowledging that religious individualism "is no more going to go away than is secular individualism") implies that social realists are in the church legitimately while the individualists are there by the social realists' sufferance. In the following quotation, in which they acknowledge that some compromise and accommodation on both sides will be required, it is easy to see that they consider the protectors of the "church idea" to be the insiders while religious individualists are the outsiders:

> It would seem that a vital and enduring religious individualism can only survive in a renewed relationship with established religious bodies. Such a renewed relationship would require change on both sides. Churches and sects would have to learn that they can sustain more autonomy than they had thought, and religious individualists would have to learn that solitude without community is merely loneliness." (*HH*, 248)

As far as their proposal for mutual accommodation itself is concerned, the suggestion that churches and sects can learn to sustain "more autonomy than they had thought" does not address the fact that, as history shows, churches and sects will inevitably come down on the side of institutional self-preservation where disputes involving religious individualism are concerned. Also, it is not that religious individualists do not understand that "solitude without community is merely loneliness," as this is the very point that expressive individualism has been making, over and over again, and that churches and sects have consistently ignored, because their organizational structures, mandates, and objectives are on a collision course with the desire of their members to be in community with one another. Far from being the cause of the absence of community within the churches and sects, individualism—as Father Morrison discovered—is the ideology that provides impetus for challenging the churches' preoccupation with organizational matters in the interests of more meaningful experiences of community. But, as Emerson pointed out, Americans have never had the courage to entrust their institutions to the theory of individualism, and the reception that *Habits* has received from the theological community indicates that it is unlikely that religious individualism will receive the churches' official endorsement any time soon. It will make itself felt surreptitiously, as when Father Morrison's parishioners have an inexplicable desire to hold themselves to a higher standard on marriage even as the church is relaxing its own standards, or when they criticize his tendency to equate the Christian faith with involvement in the organizational structure of the parish. Other names or labels will be found to explain or account for such phenomena, for, as Arieli points out, individualism is a good word that has, unfortunately, been spoiled.[24] Because it was already devalued and discredited, it proved to be a very convenient scapegoat, for who of any importance would raise a dissenting voice in behalf of such an unpopular victim?

Social Realism in the Therapeutic Ethos

One of Bellah's strongest contentions is that expressive individualism lives today in and through the therapeutic community. As he puts it, "therapy has developed an acute concern for the monitoring and managing of inner feelings and emphasizes their expression in open communication. Therapy thus continues the tradition of expressive individualism. . . ." (*HH*, 138). He notes that expressive individualists often have personal involvements in the therapeutic community and use therapeutic language to express their views about life. This language, he claims, is morally and ethically inept, as it is incapable of articulating the deeper values to which these individuals appear to adhere.

But are Bellah and his colleagues right in their view that expressive individualism is supported by the therapeutic ethos that

24. Arieli, *Individualism*, 198.

prevails today? Is the therapeutic community itself as supportive of expressive individualism as they assert? At least one major therapist, Michael P. Nichols, has challenged the assumption that the therapeutic community is committed to ontological individualism, and he laments the fact that they are not. His therapist colleagues have taken his challenge very seriously, as witnessed by the fact that his book on the subject provided the theme—"The Self in the System"—of the family therapy network conference in Washington, D.C., in 1988, which was attended by some five thousand family therapists.

The genius of family therapy was to teach us that the family is more than a collection of separate individuals, that it is a system, an organic whole whose parts function in a way that transcends their separate characteristics: "We have learned to see the unity of the system by standing back, blurring our focus on individuals in order to see the whole." However, "in the process of stepping back far enough to see the whole system, family therapists sometimes lose sight of the individual."[25] Nichols argues, therefore, that "family therapy has moved too far from the psychology of the individual, resulting in a wave of esoteric theorizing and a proliferation of mechanistic, highly technical interventions" (SS, 9).

He is especially concerned that family therapy has gone beyond using the term "system" as a metaphor, designed to help the therapist gain some kind of useful handle on a given family, to viewing the family as a system and nothing but a system:

> Early family therapists used the concepts of general systems theory as a metaphor and a model of family functioning. Describing the family as a system helped them to see that a group of interacting personalities can function like one being, a coherent composite that behaves as an irreducible unit. Families then were said to be like systems in that the behavior of every member of the system is related to and dependent on the behavior of all the others. The

25. Michael P. Nichols, *The Self in the System: Expanding the Limits of Family Therapy* (New York: Brunner/Mazel, 1987), 7.

triumph of the metaphor was so complete that we now take its presuppositions for granted. We no longer stare at family interventions with naive incomprehension; but when we compress them into a framework we impose, we are no longer free to let things be what they are. Now we fit events to a myth. (SS, 24–25)

Noting that a myth "is a construction that we forgot we constructed," Nichols says that family therapists "forget that thinking of families as systems is just one way of thinking, and we take it as a fundamental reality." To readers who protest, "But the family really *is* a system!" Nichols responds, "This simply proves my point, as this protest reveals that we have forgotten that we didn't discover reality, we invented it" (SS, 25).

While Nichols does not use the term "social realism," his criticism of the family therapy movement for having allowed a metaphor to become a fact, and a fact to become a myth, is precisely that the movement has adopted a social realist position regarding the family, that is, the family is understood to be an organization that is as real as the individuals who compose it. If family therapists merely argued that the system is no less real than the individual, this would be one thing. Quite another, and far more problematic, is that the system is considered to have ontological priority over the individual, with the result that the movement has painted "a passive picture of the self as caught up in a system that it is blind and powerless to resist" (SS, 6).

Evidence that the system is accorded ontological priority over the individual is the fact that an individual's experiences are explored only in relation to their impact on and within the system, and the fact that the power of the system is "inflated." The system, qua system, is taken to be determinative of behavior rather than just influential. Furthermore, elaborate models, with highly abstract postulates, have been put forward to explain the workings of the system. Nichols complains:

Among the wooly terms used to describe a family systems perspective are: "cybernetic epistemology," "circular epistemology," "systemic epistemology," "ecological epistemology," and "ecosystemic epistemology." These puffed-up phrases have a nice ring to them; they suggest weighty thoughts, but they cloud over the subject, surrounding it with a haze of scholarliness while actually saying little. . . . As "the new epistemology" grows ever more abstruse, clinicians lose sight of the experience-based concepts that can serve as blueprints to organize strategies in light of a family's structure. Instead, what we see in many quarters is a barrage of manipulative techniques designed to defeat a mechanical beast—"the family system." (SS, 32–33)

Nichols appeals to family therapists to wake up to the fact that, in finding the family, they are losing the self.

It is not the case, then, that the therapeutic community has been uniformly aligned on the side of individualism against social realism. If systemic theory is the dominant theory in the psychotherapeutic community today, this suggests that the therapeutic community is at least as committed to a social realist perspective as to a perspective of ontological individualism. It is entirely possible, then, that the "groping for words" that Bellah and his colleagues attribute to their interviewees' individualistic orientation is due, rather, to the fact that neither their therapeutic involvements nor their church associations have provided the language they need to articulate their desire to be a living vital self and to express their longing for some segment of the social world to confirm them in their desire to find real community in the here and now. That Nelson and others use the much overworked and over-extended word "self-fulfillment" to represent these desires, a word that is more reflective of utilitarian than expressive individualism, shows that we have great need of the rich language of expressive individualism found in the writings of Emerson a century ago and Kohut today to give voice to the deep hungers of the self and to lift up the inarticulate sighs of the oppressed soul.

6

The Making of
the Depleted Self

In *The Culture of Narcissism,* Christopher Lasch cites a study conducted by Michael Maccoby of 250 managers from twelve major companies. According to Lasch, Maccoby

> describes the new corporate leader, not altogether unsympathetically, as a person who works with people rather than with materials and who seeks not to build an empire or accumulate wealth but to experience "the exhilaration of running his team and of gaining victories." He wants to "be known as a winner, and his deepest fear is to be labeled a loser." Instead of pitting himself against a material task or a problem demanding solution, he pits himself against others, out of a "need to be in control." . . . The new executive, boyish, playful, and "seductive," wants in Maccoby's words "to maintain an illusion of limitless options." He has little capacity for "personal intimacy and social commitment."
>
> . . . In all his personal relations, [he] depends on the admiration or fear he inspires in others to certify his credentials as a "winner." (*CN*, 92–94)

It is not difficult to perceive here the perfect formula for the emergence of narcissists of the phallic and manipulative variety, the types popularly associated with the narcissism label. But, according to Lasch, the story does not end here.

> As he gets older, he finds it more and more difficult to command the kind of attention on which he thrives. He reaches a plateau

> beyond which he does not advance in his job, perhaps because the very highest positions, as Maccoby notes, still go to "those able to renounce adolescent rebelliousness and become at least to some extent believers in the organization." The job begins to lose its savor. Having little interest in craftsmanship, the new-style executive takes no pleasure in his achievements once he begins to lose the adolescent charm on which they rest. Middle age hits him with the force of a disaster: [Enter the depleted self.] "Once his youth, vigor, and even the thrill in winning are lost, he becomes depressed and goalless, questioning the purpose of his life. No longer energized by the team struggle and unable to dedicate himself to something he believes in beyond himself, . . . he finds himself starkly alone." It is not surprising, given the prevalence of this career pattern, that popular psychology returns so often to the "midlife crisis" and to ways of combating it. (*CN*, 94)

The career trajectory here is one that begins, in our twenties, with the grandiose self in the ascendancy. Then, beginning in our forties, the balloon suddenly bursts, or slowly but surely the air leaks out, leaving the self deflated and depleted. Shame is not uncommon when we experience ourselves as failures, as washed up. The idealizing self begins to speak in recriminating tones, reviewing how, had *it* been in charge all those years, things would have gone very differently. Apathy and anger also rear their ugly heads, now one, then the other, but in no predictable or discernible pattern. We slug through some days in the throes of apathy— when the idealizing self is in charge—while, other days—when the grandiose self, staggering but still on its feet, takes charge— we are fueled by inner rage.

I say "we" here because it is all too easy to join in moral condemnation of the "new-style executive," and even to take delight in the fact that he eventually gets his comeuppance, all the while failing to admit the obvious, that the enemy in this case is us. As Lasch puts it, "It is not surprising, given the prevalence of this career pattern that popular psychology returns so often to the 'midlife crisis' and to ways of combating it" (*CN*, 94).

128

What is the process by which individuals, believing that, as Maccoby puts it, they are above "being pushed around by the company," find instead that the company has the upper hand? How is the company capable of turning the individual from a grandiose self—full of illusions of limitless options—into a depleted self, feeding on and fighting with others over the few emotional scraps that fall his or her way? How does the company, the institution for which one works, accomplish this "transformation" of the self? What methods and techniques achieve this dubious outcome?

One way to get at this "transformation" of the individual into a depleted self is to focus on the major theme of individualism—personal autonomy—and to show how our social institutions are making a travesty of this noble concept, and are, in the process, undermining the essential dignity, indeed, the very sacredness, of the individual. To develop this way of viewing the issue, we begin with a brief summary of Emerson's argument for personal autonomy, and then examine the work of Richard Sennett on authority structures in modern social organizations to show how the very notion of autonomy has become a mechanism of social control, leading to the diminishment and depletion of the individual self.

The Autonomous Self

In "Self-Reliance," Emerson begins by extolling belief in one's own thoughts, in "what is true for you in your private heart" (SR, 27). There comes a time when, in our education in life, we arrive at the conviction that envy is ignorance, that imitation is suicide, and that we must take ourselves for better, for worse, as our portion and trust ourselves.

The sense of independence and freedom that results from such a conviction is analogous to "the nonchalance of boys who are sure of a dinner, and would disdain as much as a Lord to do or say aught to conciliate one." Warming to this analogy, Emerson continues:

> A boy is in the parlour what the pit is in the playhouse; independent, irresponsible, looking out from his corner on such people and facts as pass by, he tries and sentences them on their merits, in the swift summary of boys, as good, bad, interesting, silly, eloquent, troublesome. He cumbers himself never about consequences or about interests: he gives you an independent, genuine verdict. You must court him: he does not court you. (SR, 29)

This appeal to the "nonchalance of boys who are sure of a dinner" as an expression of autonomy is not surprising. As Michel Foucault points out,

> In a system of discipline, the child is more individualized than the adult, the patient more than the healthy man, the madman and the delinquent more than the normal and the non-delinquent. In each case it is towards the first of these pairs that all the individualizing mechanisms are turned in our civilization; and when one wishes to individualize the healthy, normal and law-abiding adult, it is always by asking him how much of the child he has in him, what secret madness lies within him, what fundamental crime he has dreamt of committing.[1]

How different, then, the demeanor of adults. It is, says Emerson, as though they are living in jail, for, as soon as they have once acted or spoken with conspicuous success, they become "committed" persons, worried about their reputations, and afraid to say anything that might seem to contradict what originally brought them acclaim. They become slaves to consistency, expressing great reverence for their past actions and words, largely because they are known for their past actions, and are reluctant to disappoint others who made their initial judgment about them

1. Michel Foucault, *Discipline and Punishment: The Birth of the Prison* (New York: Vintage Books, 1979), 193.

on the basis of these earlier actions. But why, Emerson asks, "should you keep your head over your shoulder? Why drag about this corpse of your memory, lest you contradict [something] you have stated in this or that public place?" After all, "a foolish consistency is the hobgoblin of little minds, adored by little statesmen and philosophers and divines. With consistency, a great soul has simply nothing to do. He may as well concern himself with his shadow on the wall. Speak what you think now in hard words, and to-morrow speak what to-morrow thinks in hard words again, though it contradict everything you said today." If you trust yourself, you need not worry that your words and actions cause misunderstanding and confusion: "Your genuine action will explain itself and will explain your other genuine actions. Your conformity explains nothing" (SR, 33–34).

To be an autonomous, independent individual, one must also be a social nonconformist, and carry oneself as though "everything were titular and ephemeral but he. I am ashamed to think how easily we capitulate to badges and names, to large societies and dead institutions." Nonconformity involves, above all else, objecting "to usages that have become dead to you," and that, if conformed to, would "scatter your force, lose your time and blur the impression of your character." One must, therefore,

> consider what a blindman's-bluff is this game of conformity. If I know your sect, I anticipate your argument. I hear a preacher announce for his text and topic the expediency of one of the institutions of his church. Do I not know beforehand that not possibly can he say a new and spontaneous word? Do I not know that with all this ostentation of examining the grounds of the institution, he will do no such thing? Do I not know that he is pledged to himself not to look but at one side,—the permitted side, not as a man, but as a parish minister? He is a retained attorney, and these airs of the bench are the emptiest affectation. Well, most men have found their eyes with one or another handkerchief, and attached themselves to some one of these communities of opinion. This conformity makes them not false in a few particulars, authors of a few lies,

but false in all particulars. Their every truth is not quite true. (SR, 32)

Emerson acknowledges that nonconformity is unpopular, and that one can be sure that the world will "whip you with its displeasure." This should not concern us, however, because the anger of the multitude has no deep cause, but blows with the wind, much as the newspapers direct. The individual should ignore public opinion and not allow it to make one timid and apologetic. The individual is in fact far more powerful than he or she imagines, for the one who is able to trust himself or herself discovers that life "has not one chance, but a hundred chances" (SR, 43).

Thus, key themes in Emerson's appeal for personal autonomy are the spontaneous freedom exhibited by children, especially in not calculating the consequences of one's actions but in cutting through appearances to the truth; the refusal to be a slave to one's past, especially that for which one became known or recognized; resistance to the demands of social conformity; and the courage to trust oneself—one's own perceptions, judgments, and the testimony of one's own experience. None of these themes suggest that Emerson equates autonomy with self-isolation, for the self who exhibits these qualities is still very much a participant in social life. That the autonomous self is involved in numerous social groups—family, work, church, and other voluntary organizations—is taken for granted. What matters is the nature of this participation. Autonomy within, not apart from, one's social involvements, is the issue. In fact, as Emerson is not an advocate of the creation of new social forms, he envisions individuals achieving such autonomy in the social groups and institutions in which they already participate.

Why, then, has Emerson been viewed by his modern critics as a proponent of self-isolation? I believe this is largely due to his criticism of those who offer help and assistance to those in need. This criticism, an often quoted section of "Self-Reliance," appears to extol a kind of utilitarian autonomy, rather than the expressive autonomy we have just described, in that everyone looks out for themselves, and care little about the needs or welfare of others. However, Emerson's criticism of those who go about helping others needs to be seen in context, as it is addressed to the "foolish philanthropist" whom he begrudges "the dollar, the dime, the cent" that he has given to "your miscellaneous popular charities," wishing that he had had the "manhood" to resist such appeals. From normal standards of human decency and compassion, this attitude of Emerson would appear indefensible, and Bellah has made this point.[2] Yet, it is based on Emerson's view that many benevolent causes do more to enhance the reputation of the philanthropist than to help those who are genuinely in need, and on his view that persons who are suffering are more helped by our expressions of confidence in their own ability to overcome their difficulties than by weeping in their presence (SR, 44–45). Of course, this view that commiserating with another does little to help is challenged by much that we know about the supportive role played by friends and relatives of those who have suffered calamities. Still, there is much truth in Emerson's point that sufferers usually have their own inner resources that are powerfully restorative if only they are able to trust themselves. Given that everyone has such inner resources, and that the problem is mainly that they do not believe in themselves, an unhealthy dependence on social institutions and agencies is unhelpful however benevolent their purposes and objectives may be.

Thus, the hero (and heroine) of "Self-Reliance" is the individual who does not "shun the ragged battle of fate, where strength is born." Compare the privileged city boy with the rural lad:

> If our young men miscarry in their first enterprises, they lose all heart. If the young merchant fails, men say he is *ruined*. If the finest genius studies at one of our colleges, and is not installed in an office within one year afterwards in the cities or suburbs of Boston or New York, it seems to his friends and to himself that he is right in being disheartened and in complaining the rest of his

2. Bellah, "The Quest for the Self: Individualism, Morality, Politics," in Paul Rabinow and William M. Sullivan, eds., *Interpretive Social Science: A Second Look* (Berkeley: Univ. of California Press, 1987), 368.

life. A sturdy lad from New Hampshire or Vermont, who in turn tries all the professions, who *teams it, farms it, peddles*, keeps a school, preaches, edits a newspaper, goes to Congress, buys a township, and so forth, in successive years, and always, like a cat, falls on his feet, is worth a hundred of these city dolls. He walks abreast with his days, and feels no shame in not "studying a profession," for he does not postpone his life, but lives already. He has not one chance, but a hundred chances (SR, 43).

As a boy, Emerson was himself deprived of love and affection by Calvinistic parents whose austere childrearing practices included depriving the children of food while the parents ate their fill (there was none of the "nonchalance of boys who are sure of a dinner" in the Emerson household!). He is therefore not an advocate of harsh or cruel treatment of others, nor does he see any inherent value in refusing to help others in time of need. But he is impressed by the resiliency of the human self, its ability to rebound from failure and to "fall on one's feet." He does not want to underestimate the inherent capacities and strengths of the individual self.

Another concern that may be raised regarding Emerson's emphasis on the autonomous self is the critique that has been made of the role that the concept of autonomy has played in developmental theory. Carol Gilligan, in her well-known book, *In a Different Voice*, was the first to assert that developmental theories, like that of Erik Erikson, describe and make normative a developmental process that is male-oriented because they locate autonomy in the initial stages of infancy or early childhood. Whereas Erikson's first developmental stage of "trust versus mistrust" anchors development in the experience of relationship, the second stage, involving the crisis of "autonomy versus shame and doubt," marks the walking child's emerging sense of separateness and agency. From then on, with each successive stage, "individuation" takes precedence over "relationship," and the process comes to its conclusion in adolescence, with "the celebration of the autonomous, initiating, industrious self through the forging of an identity based on an ideology that can support and justify adult commitments."[3] Gilligan asks, "But about whom is Erikson talking?" It is the male child, as the female child is far more oriented toward the formation of a web of relationships and interdependencies, whereas the male child is oriented toward separateness and independence. Perhaps the very fact that Emerson refers only to boys and men in "Self-Reliance" confirms her point.

On the other hand, in his own discussion of autonomy, Erikson does not talk about autonomy as separation and independence, but centers instead on the child's capacity for expressing his or her own will, and increasing judgment and decision in its application, especially in accepting the inevitable.[4] Will, according to Erikson, is "the unbroken determination to exercise free choice as well as self-restraint" when confronted by stronger or higher powers, and is thus the basis for the acceptance of law and necessity.[5] Autonomy is forged in the recognition that one has considerable opportunity to exercise free choice but is also subject to real constraints.

The question this raises is whether "will" as Erikson understands it is more reflective of male than of female development. In the "life attitudes survey" described in chap. 3, I asked laity to respond to questions concerning the virtues that Erikson ascribes to the stages of the life cycle.[6] In response to the question of whether the virtues are more characteristic of men, of women, or of both genders equally, both the men and the women identified will (defined as "the determination to overcome life's obstacles; facing life's struggles with courage, fortitude, and will") more

3. Carol Gilligan, *In a Different Voice: Psychological Theory and Women's Development* (Cambridge: Harvard Univ. Press, 1982), 11–12.
4. Erik H. Erikson, *Identity: Youth and Crisis* (New York: W. W. Norton, 1968), 112–13.
5. Erik H. Erikson, *Insight and Responsibility* (New York: W. W. Norton, 1964), 119.
6. Donald Capps, "The Deadly Sins and Saving Virtues: How They Are Viewed by Laity," in *Pastoral Psychology* 37, no. 4 (1989): 242–44.

with men than with women. Among the laymen, 35% judged it a man's virtue; 5% a woman's virtue; and 60% equal. Among the laywomen, 25% judged it a man's virtue; 11% a woman's virtue; and 65% equal. But when they were asked to indicate what virtue they personally identified with, 10% of the women and 9% of the men said they identified with will. As will functions in this study as a proxy for autonomy, it appears that autonomy is as important to women as it is to men. The view that it is more reflective of men's than women's life cycle is based on a cultural stereotype. If autonomy is considered more a man's than a woman's trait, this is because boys have been allowed or encouraged to exercise free choice, while girls have been encouraged to exercise self-restraint.

My assumption, then, is that the desire to be an autonomous self is inherent in all of us, women as well as men, and that this desire need not be understood as anti-social or anti-relational. What needs to be explored further, however, is the role modern social organizations have played in trivializing the very idea of autonomy and in betraying the deep desires and urgent longings of the self that autonomy has traditionally exemplified and represented.

Autonomy in Bureaucracies

As Lasch's analysis of the young manager indicates, most of us enter the career world with much the same attitude that Emerson espouses in his essay on self-reliance. We are determined to be our own person, not to succumb to institutional pressures to conform, not to be someone that we are not. We firmly believe that we can maintain our independence, that we will not allow ourselves to be "pushed around by the company." We are also confident that we will be able to keep our options open—our hundred chances—and that we will not get trapped by the institution and our dependence upon it. Instead, we will be able to treat it with the nonchalance of boys who are sure of a dinner: "I will not let the company get to me."

In *Authority*, Richard Sennett provides a compelling explanation for why it does not turn out this way. He, too, focuses on the managers, but in his analysis they are not the victims of the process that leaves the self demoralized and depleted. Rather, they are the ones who control the process and make it work. Thus, he presents not only a very different picture of autonomy than that which Emerson envisioned, but also a very different view of the "new-style manager" than that of Maccoby and Lasch.

Autonomy, he notes, takes a simple and a complex form. The simple form is the possession of skills that enable a person to be independent. The more complex form is one "which anyone who has worked in the upper levels of a bureaucracy will recognize," and is "a matter of character structure rather than skill." Persons are chosen to be managers on the grounds that they possess the more complex form:

> For instance, a manager is promotable not when he does just one specific task well but when he can coordinate the work of a number of people, each with his or her own expert skills. Bureaucracies have invented a whole host of images to describe the qualities of such a manager. Of course, he has to get along with other people. To direct his subordinates rather than be imprisoned by all the particular demands they make on him, however, he has to possess a set of attitudes which keep him independent, self-possessed, more influencing than reactive. This bundle of personality traits divorced of any particular technical expertise creates the complex form of autonomy. (*Auth*, 85–86)

Sennett suggests that the crucial ingredient of an "autonomous character structure" is "the ability to be a good judge of others because he or she is not desperate for their approval. Self-control thus appears as a strength, a strength of calmness and above-the-storm which makes telling others what to do seem natural" (*Auth*, 86).

Problems arise, however, when one is needed by others more than one needs them, for then one can afford to be indifferent to them. In the complex form of autonomy, keeping cool when others make demands on you or challenge you is a way of keeping the upper hand: "Of course, few people set out to be rude or callous. But autonomy removes the necessity of dealing with other people openly and mutually. There is an imbalance; they show their need for you more than you show your need for them. This puts you in control" (*Auth*, 86).

Autonomous authorities in bureaucratic organizations keep the upper hand by making the others feel ashamed. Sennett explains:

> Shame has taken the place of violence as a *routine* form of punishment in Western societies. The reason is simple and perverse. The shame an autonomous person can arouse in subordinates is an implicit control. Rather than the employer explicitly saying "You are dirt" or "Look how much better I am," all he needs to do is his job—exercise his skill or deploy his calm and indifference. His powers are fixed in his position, they are static attributes, qualities of what he is. It is not so much abrupt moments of humiliation as month after month of disregarding his employees, of not taking them seriously, which establishes his domination. The feelings he has about them, they about him, need never be stated. The grinding down of his employees' sense of self-worth is not part of his discourse with them; it is a silent erosion of their sense of self-worth which will wear them down. This, rather than open abuse, is how he bends them to his will. When shame is silent, implicit, it becomes a patent tool of bringing people to heel. (*Auth*, 95)

In effect, employees in this situation become craving and paranoid types, reduced to sulking and pouting, carping and criticizing, and issuing lame and empty threats of revenge. Shaming becomes a means of control in the hands of the one individual who is free to act autonomously.

Why do employees in such situations remain? Why do they not simply quit? In Sennett's view, autonomous authorities create a bond between themselves and their subordinates that is no less controlling than that created by authoritarian bosses. This is a bond "in which the subordinate feels a sense of dread about the attitudes of autonomy evinced by his superior, feels that mixture of fear and awe which is the most essential ingredient of authority" (*Auth*, 97). To illustrate how this "bonding" works, Sennett cites a case study that originally appeared in *Harvard Business Review* and has often been cited in management circles as "a model of how an employer should deal with a demanding employee."

Dr. Richard Dodds, a physics research worker, entered the office and showed his superior, Dr. Blackman, a letter. This letter was from another research institution, offering Dodds a position. Blackman read the letter.

Dodds: "What do you think of that?"

Blackman: "I knew it was coming. He asked me if it would be all right if he sent it. I told him to go ahead, if he wanted to."

Dodds: "I didn't expect it, particularly after what you said to me last time [pause]. I'm really quite happy here. I don't want you to get the idea that I am thinking of leaving. But I thought I should go and visit him—I think he expects it—and I wanted to let you know that just because I was thinking of going down, that didn't mean I was thinking of leaving here, unless of course, he offers me something extraordinary."

Blackman: "Why are you telling me all this?"

Dodds: "Because I didn't want you hearing from somebody else that I'm thinking of leaving here because I was going for a visit to another institution. I really have no intention of leaving here, you know, unless he offers me something really extraordinary that I can't afford to turn down. I think I'll tell him that, that I am willing to look at his laboratory, but unless there is something unusual for me, I have no intention of leaving here."

Blackman: "It's up to you."

Dodds: "What do you think?"

Blackman: "Well, what? About what? You've got to make up your own mind."

Dodds: "I don't consider too seriously this job. He is not offering anything really extraordinary. But I am interested in what he had to say, I would like to look around his lab."

Blackman: "Sooner or later you are going to have to make up your mind where you want to work."

Dodds replied sharply: "That depends on the offers, doesn't it?"

Blackman: "No, not really; a good man always gets offers. You get a good offer and you move, and as soon as you have moved, you get other good offers. It would throw you into confusion to consider all the good offers you will receive. Isn't there a factor of how stable you want to be?"

Dodds: "But I'm not shopping around. I already told you that. He sent me this letter, I didn't ask him to. All I said was that I should visit him, and to you that's shopping around."

Blackman: "Well, you may choose to set aside your commitment here if he offers you something better. All I am saying is that you will still be left with the question of you've got to stay some place, and where is that going to be?"

The discussion continued on how it would look if Dodds changed jobs at this point, and finally Dodds said:

Dodds: "Look, I came in here, and I want to be honest with you, but you go and make me feel guilty, and I don't like that."

Blackman: "You are being honest as can be."

Dodds: "I didn't come in here to fight. I don't want to disturb you."

Blackman: "I'm not disturbed. If you think it is best for you to go somewhere else, that is O.K. with me."

Again there is a lengthy exchange about what Dodds really wants and how his leaving would look to others. Finally Dodds blurts out:

Dodds: "I don't understand you. I came in here to be honest with you, and you make me feel guilty. All I wanted was to show you this letter, and let you know what I was going to do. What should I have told you?"

Blackman: "That you had read the letter, and felt that under the circumstances it was necessary for you to pay a visit to the professor, but that you were happy here, and wanted to stay at least until you had got a job of work done."

Dodds: "I can't get over it. You think there isn't a place in the world I'd rather be than here in this lab. . . ."

The purpose of the discussion seems simple. A man reports to his boss that he has been offered the possibility of another job. In the back of his mind, he is probably hoping the boss will say that his current company will match whatever outside offer the man receives. As the discussion proceeds, however, the boss responds in such a way that the man feels disloyal and guilty about even considering leaving. By the end of the interview, Dr. Dodds is in no shape emotionally to make a hardheaded decision about his own career. (*Auth*, 98–99)

What has happened here? Sennett suggests that the superior, by maintaining his own autonomy through an attitude of self-control, of calmness, of staying above the storm, has effectively controlled the whole discussion, and shamed Dodds in the process:

In the middle of their discussion Dodds says that Blackman is making him feel guilty, to which Blackman replies, "You are being as honest as can be." When one person says I feel guilty and the other responds you are being as honest as you can, they are talking on two different emotional planes. The first, the subordinate's, is about the emotions a particular discussion arouses in him; the second, the superior's, is a judgement of the whole moral character of the discussant. This judgement on the surface seems a compliment. But the approval of someone who sees beyond the moment, to make a total judgement of another person, has a cowing and subduing effect. This effect appears directly in the subordinate's next sentences: "I didn't come in here to fight. I don't want to disturb you." (*Auth*, 100)

Sennett also notes that Blackman avoids dealing with his employee on a person-to-person basis by using the technique of "reverse response." Reversed responses begin almost as soon as the discussion opens. When Dodds says that he is happy in his current job but would leave for an extraordinary offer, Blackman, instead of responding in any direct way, such as by saying, "I really want to hold on to you," or "What do you mean by 'extraordinary,' " replies, "Why are you telling me all this?" This response throws the entire burden of the conversation back on Dodds to justify himself, and Dodds reacts by trying to do so: "Because I didn't want you hearing from someone else that I was thinking of leaving here because I was going for a visit to another institution." Now the superior is clearly in control, having successfully evaded a direct reply (i.e., that he could or would make Dodds a counteroffer), and shifted the discussion to the question of whether Dodds is a loyal employee. Of course, the issue of Dodds's loyalty is not of great concern to Blackman; shifting the discussion to this issue was solely for the purpose of taking the burden off himself.

Blackman's reverse responses also succeed in reinforcing what autonomous authority is all about, namely, maintaining an attitude of dispassion and noninvolvement while the subordinate becomes increasingly emotional and distraught. The more Dodds enters the discussion, the more personally involved and personally upset he becomes. Because the boss gives nothing of himself, it is the employee who conducts his own loyalty test, with the boss maintaining the attitude that his own interests, desires, and opinions do not matter.

Such reversed responses also "tend to discredit the statements of the other party as intrinsically meaningful. When a superior says of an employee's professional prospects 'Why are you telling me all this?'—in defiance of the obvious reasons why—the employee is being told that his intentions are not revealed by what he states directly: something hidden must be the real meaning" (*Auth*, 101–2). By the end of the discussion, Dodds is reduced to asking Blackman what he should have said instead, and Blackman responds to this request, predictably, by telling Dodds how he could have acted better, all the while ignoring that his own behavior had caused Dodds to get upset. Even the way he phrased the speech that Dodds should have made—that he "wanted to stay at least until he had got a job of work done"—was a further act of shaming, for it implied that Dodds has not been around long enough to have been of any significant value to the company.

Sennett suggests that what Blackman succeeded in doing to Dodds was to elicit "infantile rage" from his employee simply by remaining, on the surface, cool and adult. Dodds is left to explain or justify himself, while Blackman has revealed nothing of himself; he does not respond to influences, he exerts them. This imbalance is his autonomy, and the bond between them is forged from this imbalance: "When Dodds first asks, Will you make it worth my while to remain here, Blackman replies by saying, You have a problem in being loyal because of the kind of person you are— unstable, grasping at opportunities, and the like. When the reversed response takes hold, the subordinate asks himself, Am I a loyal person?, not Are this man and the job worthy of my loyalty?" (*Auth*, 103). The individual in this case has been deemed to be of questionable character, and thus of questionable worth to the company.

Sennett concludes that it would be a mistake to view the employer in this case "as consciously Machiavellian. Blackman would have had to be a great actor to contrive and execute such an interview. He is instead playing according to a set of rules, following a set of assumptions, about how to deal with threats from below. These assumptions are that something other than threats will be more effective. . . . They are the same rules which make workers feel ambivalent about expressing their demands out of the conviction that their inner lives are less developed than those of their betters" (*Auth*, 104). This discussion, while dramatic, is simply part of a larger scenario in which, day after day, the employer exerts influence "as a figure of autonomous authority, influence which binds his disobedient employee to him as a potent figure whose recognition must be won" (*Auth*, 104).

It is easy to see from Sennett's analysis of this case how the conditions for narcissism are created through "autonomous authority." The effect of their discussion has been to reinforce in Dodds the craving personality, seeking affirmation but not receiving it, and, as a consequence, reduced to infantile rage and petulant sulking. It has revealed Blackman to be the manipulative personality who, through the subtle use of reverse responses, has successfully "put one over" on Dodds by toying with his aspirations and emotions. As Sennett points out, the controls that autonomous authorities exercise over others "are coming to be more veiled and protected in modern bureaucratic ideologies" (*Auth*, 88). The tyrannical authority who controlled by means of threats has been replaced by the executive who controls by exploiting the psychological bond that exists between employer and employee, using techniques of emotional manipulation.

Sennett's analysis also explains why narcissists seem to function better in the workplace than in their family lives, for, as this case reveals, two types of narcissists—the craving and the manipulative—have a bond to one another that neither, in spite of their dislike and distrust for each other, is capable of breaking. Where Emerson describes autonomy in terms of self-trust, neither Blackman nor Dodds trusts himself enough to do without the other. And so they remain "bonded" to one another, two narcissists, neither of whom is really and truly free to be himself. In fact, if one were to ask Blackman if he is a "manipulative personality" and ask Dodds if he is a "craving personality," both would vigorously deny it. To some extent, such denials would be true. The selves they have played in this discussion are false selves, which their respective roles in the institution have required them to play—indeed, roles for which the institution has provided on-the-job training.

Of the two forms of narcissism—the manipulative and the craving—the latter is especially interesting, for it relates to the question of how it is that one, in the course of a career, becomes a depleted self. An individual becomes depleted when the autonomy of the individual comes up against, and is defeated by, the autonomy wielded by the institution. (I say "the institution" because Blackman is no more truly autonomous than Dodds; he is following a set of assumptions and rules that he did not make.) The upshot is that the modern bureaucracy has made a travesty of a noble concept, that of personal autonomy, turning it into a monstrous distortion of what it meant to Emerson and other expressive individualists. This does not mean, however, that individualism is itself to blame. Rather, the blame lies with our bureaucratic institutions and the ideologues who have done to individualism what Blackman did to Dodds, that is, turned a perfectly good concept—personal autonomy—into its opposite—social control—by causing individuals to be ashamed of their legitimate desire for personal freedom, the freedom to trust themselves.

Is there any hope for such victims? Are they condemned to a future of demandingness, infantile rage, and petulant bickering, or is there some other way?

7

Countering
the Jonah Complex

*W*hen I was a boy, the pastor of our church employed the familiar "law and gospel" format in all of his sermons. The first half of the sermon would portray some facet of our sinful and hopeless condition, and the second half would focus on how God, through Christ, has redeemed us, and saved us from the sinful, hopeless condition described in the first half of the sermon. In some sermons, however, he portrayed our sinful condition so convincingly, in such a stark and depressing manner, that he was rather hard-pressed in the gospel section of the sermon to dispel the gloom he had created in the law section.

I have the same dilemma. Having devoted six chapters to exploring our narcissistic condition, will I be able, in this last chapter, to dispel the gloom that the previous chapters must surely have cast, and give readers hope that their depleted condition is not the last word, that we are not condemned to live lives hopelessly mired in the rather desperate condition portrayed in the previous chapters?

Like our law and gospel preacher, I believe I have captured and portrayed our real condition, not some fantasied condition from which no one actually suffers. If so, my task in this chapter, in its concern with "the therapeutics of the self," should not be an easy one, but should instead reflect some real struggling with the depth and seriousness of the problem, and with the real difficulties and impediments that are involved in offering hope for those who suffer from the condition of narcissism.

Unlike those who have turned to the Greek myth of Narcissus for their answers to the problem of narcissism, I have chosen the story of Jonah as my major text. This locates our concern with the therapeutics of the self in the biblical tradition. The story of Jonah also provides important insights into the narcissistic condition of the depleted self and its hopes for recovery. Unlike the myth of Narcissus, which ends in death, the story of Jonah leaves the future open, and where there is such open-endedness, there are grounds for hope. Moreover, this story offers hope because it finally self-destructs, leaving the scene open for the fresh beginning, the new start, that is portrayed in certain stories of Jesus' interaction with the depleted selves with whom he associated. If, as Heinz Kohut has contended, the task that we confront today is how to realize transformations of our narcissistic selves, I see the story of Jonah as directing our attention to our need for such transformation, and the stories in which Jesus was a healing presence as embodying such transformations.[1]

The Story of Jonah

The story of Jonah begins on an ominous note: "Now the word of the Lord came to Jonah the son of Amittai, saying, 'Arise, go to Nineveh, that great city, and cry against it; for their wickedness has come up before me.' " Nineveh was the capital city of Assyria, and to say that Hebrews, prior to the fall of Nineveh in 612 B.C.E., wanted the Assyrian Empire destroyed is a great understatement. The book of Nahum, which captures this attitude, predicts that God, being a jealous and avenging God, will lay Nineveh waste, in total desolation and ruin.

But the story of Jonah, written years after the fall of Nineveh, lacks the urgent and dreadful tone of Nahum's oracle, and is rather whimsical by contrast. Since Jonah is not a well-known and well-beloved prophet like Isaiah, Jeremiah, or Elijah, and while he

---

1. Heinz Kohut, "Forms and Transformations of Narcissism," in Morrison, ed., *Essential Papers on Narcissism*, 61–87.

may have been a historical figure (2 Kings 14:25), the author does not appear to have the usual constraints of biographers, who attempt to remain faithful, more or less, to the popular memory of a historical figure. As Elie Wiesel suggests, the author is free to make Jonah an "antihero."[2]

Jonah responds to this ominous word of the Lord by going down to Joppa, a seacoast city, paying his fare, and boarding a ship bound for Tarshish. Since Tarshish was in the opposite direction from Nineveh, he had not made the slightest pretense to heed the word of the Lord. In response to this act of independence or disobedience (call it what you will), the Lord "hurled a great wind upon the sea, and there was a mighty tempest on the sea, so that the ship threatened to break up." The mariners were afraid, each calling on his god for deliverance, and began throwing cargo overboard in order to lighten the ship's load. Meanwhile, Jonah had gone down into the inner part of the ship, lain down, and was sound asleep. The captain came down and awakened Jonah, asking him the purpose of his sleeping. Wiesel suggests that the captain may have been teasing Jonah, suggesting, in tongue-and-cheek fashion, that perhaps Jonah felt his sleeping would somehow save the ship from going under. Then, becoming serious, he asked Jonah to pray to his god for the ship's deliverance.

By casting lots, the crew determined that the cause of the evil that had come upon them was Jonah. They tried to find out what they could about him: What is your occupation? Where do you come from? What country are you from? Jonah answered that he was a Hebrew, and that the God he feared is the God who made the sea and the dry land. This response suggests a direct connection between the fact that the casting of lots pointed to Jonah and the fact that the ship was under siege: Jonah's God had made the sea and could therefore command it to do whatever he wanted. Now, everyone was very much afraid, and they said to Jonah, "What is this that you have done!" The narrator adds, perhaps

2. Elie Wiesel, *Five Biblical Portraits* (Notre Dame, Ind.: Univ. of Notre Dame Press, 1981), 137.

realizing that he had left out an important fact, "For the men knew that he was fleeing from the presence of the Lord, because he had told them."

Realizing that they were the innocent victims of a struggle between Jonah and his God, the others asked Jonah to help solve their dilemma: "What shall we do to you, that the sea may quiet down for us?" Jonah suggested that they cast him into the sea, and then the sea would quiet down for them, "for I know it is because of me that this great tempest has come upon you." But they would not accept his proposal. Whether this was because they had a responsibility to see to the safe passage of a paying customer, or because they were not entirely convinced that Jonah's God was behind this, or because they had compassion for Jonah, or some other reason, the narrator does not say. Instead, they rowed harder, trying to bring the ship back to land.

But to no avail, as the sea grew more and more tempestuous. So now they were ready to act on Jonah's suggestion. Beseeching the Lord that he would "lay not on us innocent blood"—after all, they did not know whether Jonah was guilty of serious wrong-doing—they threw Jonah into the sea, and immediately the sea "ceased from its raging." Apparently realizing that Jonah's God did in fact control the seas, they "feared the Lord exceedingly, and they offered a sacrifice to the Lord and made vows." The whole episode had made believers of them.

For all they knew, Jonah had drowned in the sea, thus satisfying its raging anger. But the Lord appointed a great fish to swallow him up, and he spent the next three days and nights in the fish's belly. While there, he prayed to the Lord. Here, the storyteller inserts a prayer for deliverance, perhaps one that was already known to his readers. (For example, this prayer has some thematic parallels with Psalm 88.) In any event, the prayer clearly attributes Jonah's original fate as well as his anticipated deliverance to the Lord, for "thou didst cast me into the deep, into the heart of the seas. . . . yet thou didst bring up my life from the Pit." Jonah's prayer ends on a note of obedience: "But I with the voice of thanksgiving will sacrifice to thee; what I have vowed I will pay. Deliverance belongs to the Lord!" Whereupon "the

Lord spoke to the fish, and it vomited out Jonah upon the dry land."

The Lord spoke to Jonah a second time, but in a rather different tone. Where the Lord's first command to Jonah was to go and cry against the city of Nineveh, this time the Lord instructed Jonah to go "and proclaim to it the message that I tell you." Jonah did as instructed, and went to Nineveh, a city so great that it took three days to journey from one end of it to the other. Jonah went about a day's journey, and cried out, "Yet forty days and Nineveh shall be overthrown!" Immediately, "the people of Nineveh believed God; they proclaimed a fast, and put on sackcloth, from the greatest of them to the least of them." The king, hearing what the people had done, did the same, covering himself with sackcloth and sitting in ashes. He then proclaimed a period of fasting and repentance, observing, "Who knows, God may yet repent and turn from his fierce anger, so that we perish not." And he was right! "When God saw what they did, how they turned from their evil way, God repented of the evil which he had said he would do to them; and he did not do it."

Though God's anger at the Ninevites subsided, Jonah's was now incited: "But it displeased Jonah exceedingly, and he was angry." In his anger, he offered an explanation for his flight to Tarshish: "I pray thee, Lord, is not this what I said when I was yet in my country? That is why I made haste to flee to Tarshish, for I knew that thou art a gracious God and merciful, slow to anger, and abounding in steadfast love, and repentest of evil. Therefore, now, O Lord, take my life from me, I beseech thee, for it is better for me to die than to live." God's response was brief: "Do you do well to be angry?" Jonah did not respond, but instead went out of the city and sat to the east of the city, and made himself a booth there. He sat under it in the shade, "till he should see what would become of the city."

Apparently feeling compassion for Jonah, God appointed a large plant to grow over him to shade his head, which pleased Jonah a great deal. But at dawn the next day, God appointed a worm that attacked the plant, and it withered. Then God appointed a sultry east wind to blow and the sun beat on Jonah's head so that he felt faint. Jonah again asked that he might die, saying, "It is better for me to die than to live." But God replied, "Do you do well to be angry for the plant?" This time Jonah did reply to God's question: "I do well to be angry, angry enough to die." Then the Lord replied: "You pity the plant, for which you did not labor, nor did you make it grow, which came into being in a night, and perished in a night. And should not I pity Nineveh, that great city, in which there are more than a hundred and twenty thousand persons who do not know their right hand from their left, and also much cattle?"

Of this ambiguous ending to the story, Elie Wiesel observes, "If indeed Jonah answered God's question, the answer has not been recorded. The book ends with God's word, which is only natural: God makes sure He has the last word, always. But, uniquely, the book ends on a question—and that is what leaves us astonished and deeply affected. How many other sacred and eternal, inspired and inspiring books are there in which the last sentence is neither affirmation nor injunction, nor even a statement, but, quite simply, a question?"[3]

Jonah—Divided, Depleted, Defensive

But are readers left "astonished and deeply affected" by their reading of the story of Jonah? God's question of Jonah at the end is so infused with the same "tongue-in-cheek" tone that Wiesel attributes to the captain of the ship—"who do not know their right hand from their left, and also much cattle"—that I find it difficult to be "deeply affected" by the story's ending on a question. Surely the narrator, by putting tongue-in-cheek words into God's mouth, is alerting the reader that the story, as a whole, is meant to be taken with a large grain of salt. Or, to put it another way, the reader is warned not to attribute more meaningfulness to this story than it deserves or can sustain." Perhaps most readers of the story have made precisely this mistake, and, as a result, have

3. Ibid., 154–55.

not fully appreciated its value for those who are personally struggling with the narcissistic condition of the depleted self.

The story of Jonah is the story of a narcissist, which may explain in part why this minor prophet has captured the imaginations of many Christians today. Contemporary readers have little difficulty seeing themselves in the main character of the story, and narcissism theory enables us to see why this is so. Jonah is not, however, the exhibitionistic or the manipulative narcissist. He is the craving narcissist throughout the story, and at the end, he has taken on characteristics of the paranoid narcissist as well. The exhibitionistic narcissist would rush to Nineveh with an attitude of reckless bravery, but Jonah did everything he could to escape what he had good reason to believe would be an experience of public humiliation; worse yet, he would be expected to act in ways that were out of character for him—incongruent with his current feelings about himself—as far more needed than needy. Anticipation of being shamed, both publicly and subjectively, led him to try to find some means of escape. There is no grandiosity here, no exaggerated sense of his self-importance. On the contrary, the Jonah that we encounter in the first scene of the story shied away from the spotlight, finding it threatening and completely out of character for him. Attention is threatening, not self-affirming. So he ran away.

But he found that allowing his shameful self to take over like this was self-defeating. On board ship, he managed to remain anonymous at the outset, but was then exposed, and therefore did not succeed in his effort to avoid being the object of attention. In an unsuccessful effort to avoid this, he gave only the most perfunctory answers to the questions put to him. He revealed his ethnic background ("I am a Hebrew") but successfully avoided the question about his profession. We cannot imagine him proclaiming with pride, "I am a prophet."

His shame also led him to offer himself as a sacrifice, as the one who must suffer so that others may live. He did not view this as a terrible fate, for to disappear, to become invisible, is much to be preferred to being the center of attention. This feeling—"I'd rather die than speak before the Ninevites"—is not at all difficult for narcissists with a well-developed sense of shame to appreciate. In a recent national poll, the fear of public speaking was ranked first among dreaded experiences, while fear of death ranked only sixth. Clearly, for many of us, experiences in which we are the object of attention, experiences that hold the distinct likelihood that we will be shamed, are more dreadful even than death itself. Death, in fact, would come as a welcome relief.

But for Jonah, there was no saving death. For those prone to shame, and dreading the shameful event that lies somewhere in the near or distant future, there is no such relief. He realized, therefore, that he had better accept the fate that he had sought to escape by running away. This decision to face the future he so much dreaded is a reaction against his shameful self. Aware that avoidance had not worked, that one survives in spite of one's desire to die, he turned against his shameful self. He said, in effect, "I am better than my shameful self has represented me to be, has permitted me to be, and I will no longer allow it to dictate my decisions in life. Instead, I will do what my shameful self has been trying to protect me from having to do."

This resolve reveals little grandiosity such as we would expect from the exhibitionistic narcissist. The tone of his prayer for deliverance, with its vow to do what he needed to do, does not express any reckless bravado. He was instead responding with his idealizing self, with what he viewed as his better, more mature, more adult self. Since the idealizing self reflects the internalization of the ideals that one has derived from others, to attribute his determination to go to Nineveh to his idealizing self is consistent with the narrator's suggestion that Jonah's going to Nineveh was God's idea, and that in agreeing to go Jonah was no longer disobeying the will of God. So concerned was Jonah to heed the idealizing self that he did not express whatever doubts he still must have had about his role in Nineveh, nor did he ask how he might go about preparing for Nineveh so that the experience of shame he so much dreaded might be less likely to occur. In other words, the idealizing self silences all the questions he might otherwise have asked about why he had been tapped for the job, what made him the best choice, and, if he really must be the appointed one, how might he improve his chances of succeeding? If he were not reacting so much against his shame—the shame of cowardice and flight—he would probably have had the necessary self-esteem to raise these doubts and questions, and not have felt that they would only reveal him for the sorry person he really is.

Instead, in a resolute frame of mind, he went to Nineveh, and did as he believed he was expected to do, speaking the words that he believed he had been charged to speak. The people of Nineveh evidently perceived that these were not his words, the words he would have said were he speaking only for himself, for we are told that they believed not Jonah but God. The idealizing self was in command during his brief tenure as prophet to Nineveh.

On the surface, he was successful: the people responded to what he was saying, and did what was necessary to avert the fate they dreaded. It is not surprising, however, that he was unhappy with his success, for there was no mirroring between himself and the people of Nineveh. True, he avoided shame—he got through the performance without totally embarrassing himself—but there was no pleasure in it: the exhilaration of connecting with his listeners, and receiving admiration and approval from the Ninevites for mirroring to them their inner thoughts and feelings. "And they believed God" speaks volumes about what did *not* happen in Nineveh between Jonah and the people.

The result was altogether predictable: he felt depleted, emotionally empty. He was also angry. The grandiose self that had been suppressed during his mission to the Ninevites now asserted itself in a reckless display of anger directed to God. God had set him up and let him down. God had played false with him. God had exploited his determination to play his role as he was supposed to play it, and had shamelessly used him. Suddenly in the ascendancy, his grandiose self overreached, attributing his original decision to flee to Tarshish not to his shameful self—the real reason he fled—but to his thoroughly rational thought processes: See, this is why I fled in the first place, for I knew this would happen if I went. This is the grandiose self speaking now, and what it says is clearly specious, for the story does not mention that Jonah had raised these objections prior to escaping to Tarshish, or even before going to Nineveh. Only now, in his grandiose state, was he able to express these objections.

The grandiose self, then, fueled by inner rage, resorted to the strategy of the transfer of blame, making God responsible for his flight to Tarshish. His sudden, vaulting burst of grandiosity also enabled him to express his deep contempt for the Ninevites, a people hardly worth saving. In this way, he externalized his own shame by adopting a judgmental, faultfinding, or condescending attitude toward others. While he did not openly voice such contempt, he implied it in his sarcastic words about God being a merciful God who is slow to anger, etc. Only a God who does not mind being manipulated by acts of false repentance would repent of the evil he planned for this contemptible group of people. Thus, in his reaction to what occurred in Nineveh, Jonah's grandiose self took charge, exploding against God and resorting to defensive strategies designed to draw attention away from his shameful self. Such grandiosity could not, however, conceal the deep and painful self-depletion that he felt after his mission to Nineveh.

God as Autonomous Authority

While some interpreters have raised questions about some of God's actions in the story, all have come to God's defense, and viewed the God portrayed in the story as the God in whom Christians should—and do—believe.

Richard Sennett's analysis of autonomous authority—what he calls "authority without love"—challenges this. In my view, God functions in the story of Jonah as an autonomous authority. Autonomous authorities make use of shame as a means of maintaining control over a subordinate. This does not require the employer to say explicitly, "You are dirt," or "Look how much better I am"; instead, all he or she needs to do is to display calm and indifference, and thereby effect a "silent erosion of their sense of self-worth" (*Auth*, 95). In the case of Dr. Blackman and Dr. Dodds, Blackman used the technique of reverse response to throw the entire burden on Dodds to justify himself, thus enabling Blackman to remain firmly in control. As Dodds became more and more upset with Blackman's failure to respond directly, and with his patronizing attitude of wanting to "help" Dodds sort out his feelings about his loyalty to the company, Dodds succumbed to infantile rage.

This is essentially how God treated Jonah, especially after the episode in Nineveh. Instead of praising Jonah for his role in Nineveh and explaining to Jonah why he relented and did not carry through on his threat to destroy the Ninevites, he placed the burden on Jonah to justify himself: "Do you do well to be angry?" By not answering God at that moment, Jonah temporarily avoided the fate of Dodds, but this was short-lived. Causing a plant to grow and shield Jonah, and then appointing a worm to destroy the plant the very next day, God manipulated Jonah's emotions, subjecting him to a kind of psychological whiplash against which Jonah, in his depleted state, had no defense. Then, God again raised the question of Jonah's anger, this time relating it not to what had happened in Nineveh but what had just happened to the plant, thereby directing the discussion away from anger relating to a significant event to anger over a smaller, more trivial one. Now, when Jonah responded to the question of the appropriateness of his anger, his anger seems infantile and childish, petulant and immature.

God was quick to seize the advantage that Jonah's petulant response afforded him. First, he rubbed it in: "You pity the plant, for which you did not labor, nor did you make it grow." Then, he taught Jonah a lesson in compassion: "And should not I pity Nineveh, that great city, in which there are more than a hundred and twenty thousand persons. . . ." Thus, God did not have to tell Jonah, "You are dirt," or "Look how much better I am." He needed only to turn the tables on Jonah by asking the seemingly innocent question: "Do you do well to be angry?" Now the issue is not God's decision to save Nineveh and the effect of this decision on Jonah, but Jonah's character: the fact that he had an angry streak, and seemed unable to maintain the calm and above-the-storm demeanor, not to mention the magnanimity, that God displayed. Moreover, Jonah's anger concerned not only what happened to him in Nineveh, but also petty and trivial issues like a plant dying. This use of reverse response leaves God well above the storm and is beautifully calculated to grind Jonah down, to break his independent spirit. By the end of the story, he was hardly any different from those other creatures of God—the raging sea, or, perhaps more analogously, the grimy little worm—who automatically and unthinkingly did God's bidding. True, he argued against God, as Dodds argued with Blackman, but, in the end, he was no less demoralized. His voicing of objections only proved how much he was in God's control. He is reduced to petulance and whining. Whatever happened to the autonomous self, to the nonchalance of boys who are sure of a dinner?

Of course, some would argue that God skillfully brought Jonah to the point where he could hear and respond to the lesson that God had wanted to teach him, a lesson about mercy and compassion. They would say that Jonah had to go through the experience of losing his plant so that he would get the point about compassion for others, even those for whom one might feel contempt. In this way, the plant episode is a parable. But, if this is so, God's use of the plant to teach Jonah a valuable lesson in life is rather heavy-handed, for the analogy drawn between God and the Ninevites and Jonah and his plant functions precisely opposite to a parable. A parable shatters one's customary ways of looking at life, turning upside down one's usual ways of perceiving reality, and is precisely not intended to teach a moral lesson. Thus, what God has done here is not to have functioned parabolically, but moralistically, much as Blackman did when he forced Dodds to take a closer look at his own character and to ask himself whether he was capable of being truly loyal to anything besides himself.[4]

4. In his analysis of the parable of the Good Samaritan, John Dominic Crossan argues that the parable is not told to teach a moral lesson about helping a neighbor in distress, but to turn our normal manner of perceiving the world upside down. See *In Parables* (New York: Harper & Row, 1973), 63–66. He treats the story of Jonah as a parable in *The Dark Interval* (Niles, Ill.: Argus Communications, 1975), 72–77.

God's response to Jonah is thus a patent example of the exercise of autonomous authority for the purpose of shaming a subordinate, and, in the process, raising large doubts concerning the subordinate's character. But Sennett's view that it would be a mistake to consider the employer, in the case of Blackman and Dodds, as consciously Machiavellian also applies to the God of the story of Jonah. God, it would appear, was playing according to a set of assumptions and rules about how to deal with one's subordinates. These assumptions and rules are designed to make subordinates feel ambivalent about expressing their demands out of the conviction that their inner lives are less developed than that of the employer. Thus, if Jonah's inner life were as developed as God's, it would have been obvious to him that God acted correctly when he allowed the Ninevites to survive, and he would certainly not have given in to the petulant rage that he displayed over the Nineveh experience and the withered plant. Moreover, since God is Jonah's superior in terms of moral probity and depth, Jonah is bound to him as a potent figure whose recognition must be won. By the end of the story, then, Jonah is more bound to God than ever before, in spite of—indeed, because of—the fact that God has put him through a terribly humiliating experience in Nineveh and has, subsequently, toyed with his feelings with a condescension that Jonah (unlike the Ninevites) does not deserve. After all, unlike the Ninevites, Jonah tried his best to represent God faithfully and courageously in Nineveh.

Some may argue that God's response to Jonah was not condescending but playful. There is obvious humor in God's observation that the Ninevites do not know their right hand from their left, and in his suggestion that if the people of Nineveh were destroyed, much cattle would also be destroyed, implying that the loss of cattle would be the real tragedy. But, playful and teasing as God's response may be, the fact remains that God put Jonah through a terribly humiliating experience in Nineveh, and one would have hoped that God would treat Jonah with a bit more of the compassion he claims to have felt toward the Ninevites. Surely Jonah deserved this much. But, as Sennett suggests, autonomous authority is sadly deficient in love. The bond it creates is based, instead, on the superior's ability to maintain a cool and passionless calm, and on the subordinate's acceptance of inner shame—a perfect prescription for the depleting of the self.

Waking Up from a Bad Dream

The storyteller portrays Jonah as a man who sleeps, who therefore deals with his problems through withdrawal. He slept in the inner part of the ship while all hell was breaking loose around him, and he apparently slept during the night after his frustrating day in Nineveh. Given the fact that sleeping plays a role within the story of Jonah, perhaps it is not too farfetched to suggest that the story be read as a dream—Jonah's dream—and that the only real solution to Jonah's problems is that he wake up and say, with obvious relief, "It was only a dream."

We have noted that persons who have had a particularly traumatic experience of shame express the vain hope that they are dreaming, that they will soon wake up and realize that it never happened. Perhaps instead of continuing to try to justify the actions of the God who is portrayed in the story, we need to have the courage to say that the whole thing is a very bad dream, a nightmare, and that Jonah's salvation lies in his ability to perceive that this is a dream from which he can and must wake up. The raging sea, the monster fish, the miraculous plant, the ravenous worm—these are the stuff of which dreams, bad dreams, are made. And so is the God who would treat a person as the God in the story treated Jonah.

If this is all a bad dream, then the conflict it portrays between Jonah and God is all in Jonah's head, a conflict reflecting a hopelessly divided self, with now one, now another self in temporary, tenuous control. As a dream, the story reveals Jonah's unsuccessful efforts to integrate these selves. On an even deeper level, it reveals his failure to give any consideration to the real self that is deeply embedded beneath his false self, much like the inner part of the ship to which he took refuge as the sea raged wildly and uncontrollably around him. Even now, this real self remains elusive, beyond his grasp. Is it any wonder, then, that at the end of the dream, he is depleted, longing to die, and that God—the voice of the idealizing self—gets the last word after the grandiose self has acted out, and tells Jonah that his victimization was the necessary price that had to be paid to save human society: "And should not I pity Nineveh?" Or, as Blackman might put it, "How can I run a company if I cave in to the demands of every employee?" To which Jonah can only sigh the sigh of the oppressed creature.[5]

In other words, Jonah's salvation—the discovery of his true self—will not come from remaining within the frame of this story, but by breaking out of it and entering a wholly different frame.[6] Even as Dodds's situation was hopeless to the extent that he lived within the frame of his relationship with Blackman, so Jonah cannot hope to discover the self that he truly is by remaining within a situation in which he is the victim of the autonomous authority of God, an authority without love. His rescue from the great fish is no deliverance at all if it means being saved only to be victimized again. Surely the self that is revealed in and through his victimization is not his true self, but a defensive self, a self created to defend itself against further depletion, but not a self that has its own center of initiative, that knows and follows its own course.

5. In *Reframing*, I offered a different view on the story of Jonah, viewing his situation as more comic than tragic, using Paul Watzlawick's phrase, "the situation is hopeless but not serious," to unlock the story. In offering this more tragic interpretation, I am not retracting the previous interpretation, as I believe that the text allows for both interpretations, though not simultaneously. As Freud showed in *Jokes and Their Relation to the Unconscious* (New York: Norton, 1963), jokes and dreams employ similar techniques, and reveal (and conceal) similar unconscious thoughts and motives. I leave it to readers to decide whether the story, for them, is akin to joke or to dream, depending, I would assume, on their personal circumstances. Beyond the scope of our present inquiry is the whole question of what the story meant to Jesus as he considered his own relationship to God (see his use of the figure "the sign of Jonah" in Matthew 12:38-41; 16:4). See *Reframing: A New Method in Pastoral Care* (Minneapolis: Fortress Press, 1990), 178–81.

6. Ibid., 9–13.

Jonah's life alternatives, once he leaves the frame of the story, are uncertain; the narrator does not envision Jonah living a life other than his current life as the prophet of God. But, if the ancient Jonah seems to have no alternative but to suffer victimization at the hands of a God who shows more concern and mercy for Nineveh than for Jonah, we modern Jonahs can refuse to be victimized in this way, and can take alternative life courses. We can say that surely a God who causes us to construct a false self and to deny our true self is a false God, a God we can—and must— do without. Dodds's relationship to Blackman demonstrates how difficult it is to recognize, much less break, the asymmetrical relationships that shame creates and sustains. How much more difficult it is for one to relinquish such a relationship where God is the "other." Acknowledging that one has been serving a false God is terribly difficult, and one would therefore expect the same reactions that accompany the discovery that the false self one has constructed is no longer tenable: panic, emptiness, and a deep sense of shame for having given oneself to one who did not deserve such sacrifice, and who did not give of himself in return.

At the same time, this discovery, painful as it is, provides a clearing, a new sense of being able to hear and to see clearly for the first time, without the distortion that, in Emerson's words, is not "false in a few particulars, but false in all particulars." It leaves one free to enter into experiences in which the old authority dynamics, with their subtle methods of control through shaming, have been replaced by a new form of authority, and hence, a new construal of the relationship of self and other.

Have Faith in Yourself

Another biblical text envisions this alternative. It relates an episode in which the potential was great for someone to be ground down even further, but who, through the deft intervention of the authority figure, experienced affirmation—positive mirroring— instead. This is the story of the woman, "a woman of the city, who was a sinner" (Luke 7:36-50). She brought an alabaster flask of ointment, and standing behind Jesus, "began to wet his feet with her tears, and wiped them with the hair of her head, and kissed his feet, and anointed them with the ointment." Jesus did not resist her attentions, knowing that by allowing her to idealize him, her own sense of self would be strengthened and become more secure, free, and self-trusting. What could do more to lift her spirits, as she had lifted his, than his response to critics who said that he, a prophet, should have been able to see that she was a woman of the streets, or should have insisted that the ointment be sold and the proceeds given to the poor: "Why do you trouble the woman? For she has done a beautiful thing to me" (Matt. 26:10). What could do more to inspire her to a life no longer dominated by shame and insatiable neediness than his prediction, "Wherever this gospel is preached in the whole world, what she has done will be told in memory of her" (Matt. 26:13), and his benediction, "Your faith has saved you; go in peace" (Luke 7:50).

Jesus refused to allow this episode to degenerate into the meaningless discussion to which Blackman subjected Dodds about the quality of his character, and into which Jesus' critics sought to draw him, but instead kept the focus on the central issue: the self and its fight for survival. The key words here are "Your faith has saved you." Her behavior toward him—the beautiful thing that she did—was an act of self-trust, for she would not have done this thing for him had she not believed in herself enough to take the first step. Self-trust was manifest in her act of calling attention to herself by bestowing her loving attention on him. Her faith in Jesus was confirmed for her when he spoke approvingly of her faith in herself. His message to the depleted self who came to him that night was simple: Have faith in yourself. These were words she had not heard from anyone else, yet had longed to hear from someone who merited her trust.

If Jesus was able to recognize her act for what it truly was— an act of self-affirmation—this must surely have been because, though born in the shame of illegitimate birth,[7] he nonetheless

7. See Jane Schaberg, *The Illegitimacy of Jesus: A Feminist Theological*

had experiences as a boy or young man in which his own belief in himself was graciously, powerfully affirmed. Perhaps it happened when he was twelve and decided to remain behind in Jerusalem to talk with the teachers. For what could have done more to affirm his faith in himself than to find the teachers so affirming of him? As Luke puts it, his parents found him "sitting among the teachers, listening to them and asking them questions; and all who heard him were amazed at his understanding and his answers" (2:46-47). That he had worried his parents sick was as irrelevant as the fact that the ointment the woman used to anoint Jesus' feet could have been sold and the proceeds given to the poor. There will always be worried parents. The chance to have one's faith in oneself confirmed is a rare opportunity, and Jesus—for his own self's sake—could not afford to miss it. His faith had saved him, and he could go in peace.

Here, in the story of the woman who was a sinner, the relationship of self and other was not based on shame, but mutual self-trust, which enabled both to affirm the goodness of the other, and to do so without the sense of shame that usually accompanies such episodes. It would have been easy for Jesus to have responded to the woman's actions with embarrassment, and to have taken such embarrassment out on her. He could easily have shamed her, using any one of the defensive strategies that we have at our disposal in such situations. He could have been contemptuous of her, treating her as the sinful woman that she was, knowing that no one in the company would have dared speak up if he had chosen to humiliate her. Or he could have taken immediate and self-protective control of the situation by quickly ushering her out of the room, and, returning to his male friends, making a joke about this poor emotionally starved woman who was unable to control her emotions and to keep her hands off of

---

Interpretation of the Infancy Narratives (San Francisco, Calif.: Harper & Row, 1987). As Schaberg focuses on the implications of the illegitimacy for Mary, I have discussed its implications for Jesus in "Religion and Child Abuse: Perfect Together," *Journal for the Scientific Study of Religion* 31 (1992): 1–14.

him. That he did none of these things, but allowed her to carry out her simple, heartfelt ceremony, is testimony not only to his own goodness as an individual, but also to the fact that he was ushering in a new age in self-other relationships, having a new set of rules, a new set of assumptions, based in a new kind of bonding that can be described only as a bonding in *love*. The unbalanced, asymmetrical relationship based on the bond of shame, where one individual's inner self is judged to be inherently inferior to that of the other, is replaced by relationships based on the bond of love, where each inner self is beautiful to the eyes of the other.

Beheld and Beholding

Another gospel text that makes much the same point, that Jesus ushered in a new era, replacing the bond of shame with the bond of love, is found only in the Gospel of John (19:26-27). The scene is the crucifixion, and, more specifically, the painful and awkward conversation between the one who is dying and those who are left to survive, and carry on, as best they can. Seeing his mother and the disciple whom he loved standing near, Jesus said to his mother, "Woman, behold your son!" and to the disciple, "Behold, your mother!" To which the narrator adds, "And from that hour the disciple took her to his own home." Here again, a bond of love is established between two individuals, and it is accomplished, as in the previous story, through the positive mirroring of one another.

Positive mirroring engenders love, and of such love community is born. It is often suggested that the Christian community began with the resurrection of Christ, with the disciples' realization that he who was dead is now alive. But, according to the Gospel of John, for those who loved Jesus the most deeply—the group of mourners gathered around the cross—it began before he breathed his last breath, as a woman and a man beheld one another, and saw, in that moment, what the one on the cross had seen in the other. In that moment, a bond of love was established, a bond much stronger than shame, the death we die daily. By inviting them to behold one another, even as he was, even then, beholding them, Jesus exercised a new kind of authority, and ushered in a new era in human relating.

The hunger of the depleted self is, at root, the hunger for loving and being loved. This comes as no great mystery, and is hardly a startling or novel conclusion. But these two stories involving Jesus suggest a different fate for the depleted self than the story of Jonah, where the self remains divided, defensive, and depleted because it is caught up in an asymmetrical relationship in which the authority of the one is built on the shame of the other. These two stories also reveal that our real self is not inaccessible, but we need the assistance of another to find it. Our real self is discovered through the recognition that we receive from one another, in the moment that our self-affirmation is affirmed by the other. The source of self-knowing is not private introspection but the mutual mirroring of selves.

Unlike the story of Jonah, these two stories have nothing to say directly about God. But this need not concern us, because the reason for this is that God is not a character in these stories, but is instead the stories' action or plot. As Paul Ricoeur points out in his sermon on the parables of Jesus, the kingdom of God "is not compared to the man who . . . to the woman who . . . to the yeast which . . . but to *what happens* in the story."[8] God is what happens in the stories, and is therefore revealed in the fact that a woman came to believe in herself because someone believed in her, and in the fact that two individuals were able to behold one another because they had been beheld by a third. Such a God does not need a name, like a character in a story. But, in this context, we can say that, like the son and friend who had one last gift to bestow before he died, God is the one who authorizes and underwrites our mutual beholdings, thus breaking the vicious

8. Paul Ricoeur, "Listening to the Parables of Jesus," in *The Philosophy of Paul Ricoeur*, ed. Charles E. Reagan and David Stewart (Boston: Beacon Press, 1978), 240.

cycle of self-repair that had produced only more, not less, self-depletion.

Self-Care as Moral Imperative

What are the implications of our interpretations of these gospel stories for the Christian community today? These stories make clear that the central concern of Jesus in face-to-face encounters was to focus attention on the self and its heroic struggle to survive. Aware that, in his younger years, he himself had been an endangered self, Jesus was conscious of the dangers of self-loss. He was unusually responsive to those who were seeking ways to discover and affirm their true selves, and was not put off by the unusual and unorthodox methods they devised for this. These were persons who would not accede to self-depletion, to self-loss, but were determined to have a self, to become the self they were destined to be. These were the persons to whom Jesus was positively attracted, and to whom he pointed as examples of saving faith.

In "Technologies of the Self," Michel Foucault notes that early Greek and Roman philosophers developed the moral principle of "taking care of oneself," and suggests that this was an important theme in early Christianity as well. But, in time, the idea that self-care is a moral imperative was challenged, basically on the grounds that it is "difficult to base rigorous morality and austere principles on the precept that we should give ourselves more care than anything else in the world."[9] Agreeing with this skeptical view of self-care as a moral imperative, Christian asceticism introduced the counter-precept of self-renunciation and institutionalized the practice of bearing witness against oneself. In time, the ideal of self-care was replaced with self-exposure, and the

9. Michel Foucault, "Technologies of the Self," in Luther H. Martin, Huck Gutman, and Patrick H. Hutton, eds., *Technologies of the Self: A Seminar with Michel Foucault* (Amherst, Mass.: Univ. of Massachusetts Press, 1988).

resulting self-revelations were for the purpose of abasing, nullifying, and even destroying the self. Before long, the Christian ascetic tradition led to the relinquishing of control of the self to the direction of another (i.e., a spiritual director), and hence to the self's domination and diminishment.

If our analysis of what is happening to the self in our narcissistic age is at all accurate, then it would seem that the Christian ascetic tradition has been all too successful, and that the time has come for us to recognize that taking care of our selves—this once-in-a-lifetime gift—is emphatically not a self-indulgence, but a moral imperative.

Emerson's essay on self-reliance is a passionate endorsement of this imperative, for it was clear to him that the despairing sigh of the oppressed creature will become, in time, the rattle of death. For him, the initial step in self-recovery is the simple affirmation that I am a self: "Few and mean as my gifts may be, I actually am, and do not need for my own assurance or the assurance of my fellows any secondary testimony" (SR, 31). Such self-affirmations may be condemned, as the Christian ascetic tradition has done, as unseemly "celebrations" of the self: as shameless expressions of personal hubris, of selves that are too full of themselves. But this is hardly the problem experienced by the depleted self, who, engaged in a fight for survival, has little to celebrate, and much to lament and decry.

The gospel stories also suggest that such self-affirmation needs itself to be affirmed, and that this is where the self has need of other selves, especially other selves who recognize that such self-affirmations are not the grandiose antics or defensive maneuvers of the narcissistic self, but legitimate appeals for self-recognition. This is where the religious community plays a vital role. As Erik Erikson suggests, our self-affirmation—our claim to be a self—is sustained by "brothers and sisters in God" who "appoint each other true '*You*'s in mutual compassion and joint veneration. The Hindu greeting of looking into another's eyes—hands raised close to the face with palms joined—and saying, 'I recognize the God in you' expresses the heart of the matter."[10] The scene at the cross also expresses the heart of the matter: They beheld one another, and from that very hour he took her into his home. To struggle against what Erikson calls "that unbearable prejudice against the self"[11] is to carry on the work of Jesus in any age. This is as true as ever in the age of the depleted self.

10. Erik H. Erikson, *Identity: Youth and Crisis* (New York: W. W. Norton, 1968), 220–21.
11. Erik H. Erikson, *Toys and Reasons: Stages in the Ritualization of Experience* (New York: W. W. Norton, 1977), 95.

Index

Scripture

Subjects and Authors